ORANGES & LEMONS

Sarah Woodward

Photography by Diana Miller

conran
OCTOPUS

CONTENTS

Photographs:
Previous pages: Mussel & Lemon Salad (see page 41)
and Tagliolini al Limone (see page 72)
Left: Black Olives with Orange Zest (see page 130)

INTRODUCTION

"IT IS HARD TO ENVISAGE ANY COOKING WITHOUT LEMONS" wrote Elizabeth David in the 1950s, her palate still scarred from the absence of lemons in Britain during the war years. I would extend that typically sweeping statement to include oranges as well—the golden fruit, the Spanish call them. As the nursery rhyme goes, "Oranges and lemons, say the bells of St. Clement's," and these days I happen to live directly opposite St. Clement's Hospital. But the two fruits were linked together in my mind from childhood years spent in Italy, for oranges and lemons are also the very essence of the Mediterranean, where I first learned to care about food.

The Mediterranean is unthinkable without its orange and lemon trees. They shape not just the food but the very landscape. Some of the citrus groves that so delight the eye date back hundreds of years, but citrus fruits are not indigenous to the area. Oranges and lemons are believed to have originated in the eastern Himalayas and to have arrived on Mediterranean shores from China and India. The Romans bought bitter oranges from Arab traders, who in turn had brought them from the fabled East, but the Mediterranean truly owes its citrus fruit orchards to the invasion by the Moors of North Africa.

By the sixteenth century oranges and lemons had become prized across Europe—for their perfume as much as for their flavor. Wealthy noblemen and women alike carried orange peel in delicate silver filigree containers to mask the rank odors of the street. Elizabeth David reports that in 1533 the Company of Leathersellers paid six silver pennies for a single lemon to offer at a banquet for the newly crowned queen Anne Boleyn.

And when Christopher Columbus made his second voyage to the New World at the end of the fifteenth century, he was quick to load oranges and lemons on board at the Canary Island of Gomera, so that groves could be established on Hispaniola, in the Caribbean. From there it was but a short hop for the citrus fruit to arrive on the American mainland.

LEFT *Lemons growing on the steep coastal terraces that rise above the medieval villages of Italy's Cinque Terre region, south of Genoa. Italy is home to some of the world's best lemons.*

ABOVE *Harvesting lemons in Cyprus. Today citrus groves are synonymous with the Mediterranean landscape, but lemons and oranges are thought to have come originally from the East.*

OPPOSITE *Fresh oranges piled high at a juice stall in Marrakesh's famous Djemaa el Fna market. Oranges—and lemons—are an important ingredient of Moroccan cuisine.*

The names by which oranges in particular are known around the world indicate the travels that the fruit has undertaken. Until comparatively recently in California the sweet orange was called the Portugal or the Malta orange, while in the local Neapolitan dialect today oranges are still called *portugales.*

However, it is the Spanish name for orange, *naranja,* that reveals the earliest history of the fruit: In ancient Sanskrit, the language of the East, the orange was known as *narunga,* which became *naranji* amongst the Arab seafarers who first brought the fruit to European shores. It became *aurantium* in Latin and, later, *arancia* in Italian, finally turning into "orange" in both French and English.

Evidence of their origins are also seen in the names of particular varieties of orange. For example, the bitter orange—which is used mainly to make marmalade—is more commonly known as a Seville orange, after the Andalusian city where it was first planted by the Moors; and one of the well-known varieties of blood orange is the Moro, from "Moor."

Today, when our supermarket shelves are piled high with oranges and lemons all year round, it is easy to forget what a treasure they once were.

Perhaps as a direct result of their lack of scarcity value, we tend to take oranges and lemons far too much for granted in our kitchens, not giving them the pride of place they undoubtedly deserve. A bowl of oranges and lemons on the kitchen table is still one of the most alluring sights I know. Once upon a time they were so precious that they would have been left there simply to fill the room with their wonderful fragrance. Now we are lucky enough to be able to use oranges and lemons with abandon at each and every stage of the meal.

ORANGES & LEMONS
IN THE KITCHEN

There are many dishes which, although they would not be the same without an orange or a lemon, need simply to be served with a quarter or two of the fruit to produce the required effect. I remember a charcoal-broiled chicken served in Egypt with nothing but a little pile of coarse salt, some toasted cumin seeds, and a plate of lemon quarters; a pork chop cooked over a wood fire in Valencia and served with half an orange to squeeze over the meat; and, of course, there are the countless times I have enjoyed a charcoal-broiled fish with nothing more that a fat, juicy lemon. These are happy memories of simple pleasures, but they are not what this book is about. Except for a few recipes where the addition of a final squeeze of orange or lemon juice falls outside our normal culinary practice, I have concentrated on recipes where the orange or lemon forms an integral part of the dish itself.

We may be used to lemons in savory dishes, but we tend to associate oranges with desserts. Not so in the Mediterranean. A Provençal daube of beef is never prepared without a sliver of dried orange peel, which gives a haunting flavor to the resulting stew; and fishermen in Greece throw their orange peel into *kakavia*, the fish soup from which Italian *zuppa di pesce* and French *bouillabaisse* are direct descendants.

Even English cookbooks from the seventeenth and eighteenth centuries show that orange juice and zest were used to flavor soups and stews, to finish little dishes of meat or fish simmered over the open fire, to embellish sauces, and, of course, for those marvelous desserts and preserves.

Both oranges and lemons are catalysts to flavor. Chicken broth is, well, boring, but add eggs and lemon and you have the exquisite Greek soup avgolémono. An insipid tomato sauce takes on a new dimension with the addition of orange zest and juice, especially if you do not have the fat, juicy tomatoes of Provence, which is where this practice comes from. They are also antidotes to richness—orange juice makes all the difference to spinach cooked with cream and butter, and lemon juice perfectly counteracts the fattier meats. A bitter orange sauce with roast duck or a pat of lemon-and-parsley butter on a broiled steak proves the point.

Oranges and lemons have found their place in kitchens all around the world, but for me they are used to best effect in their first adopted home, the Mediterranean. The cooks of the Mediterranean generally take the simple approach, relying on the best of ingredients. And we should do the same.

VARIETIES OF ORANGE & LEMON

Lemons

Lemons differ vastly in the thickness of their zest and pith, their size, the knobbliness of their skin, and the sweetness (or otherwise) of their juice, but although they come in many different varieties, they all belong to the same family. Most lemons are acidic, but there are also hybrid lemons that are sweet. In my opinion, the very best sweet lemons are grown around the rocky shores of the Mediterranean above Amalfi, and in Sicily. They have a thin zest but lots of pith and are so sweet that you can suck them like an orange. They are in season during January and February, but are hard to find in our markets. Other sweet varieties are the Marrakesh limonette, the Millsweet, and the Meyer—a cross between a lemon and an orange. As much of the point of a lemon lies in its zest, which harbors its essential oils, as in the juice. Whenever you are using lemon zest in your cooking, use unwaxed lemons, for their flavor and to avoid unnecessary chemicals.

ABOVE *Oranges are often picked underripe because they have long journeys ahead of them. Left to ripen fully on the tree, they are easier to peel and far more fragrant.*
OPPOSITE *Harvested lemons languish in a sunny spot overlooking Italy's stunning Amalfi coastline. This part of Italy is famed for its wonderfully sweet lemons.*

Oranges

The common sweet orange comes in a huge number of varieties, as I found on my visit to the Orange Museum in Burriana, near Valencia, the Spanish city that has given its name to the best-known type. According to food historian Alan Davidson, however, the much-loved, juicy "Valencia late" (late season) orange originates not in Spain but in the Azores, and other historians have also strongly suggested

Portuguese origins. Certainly, its cultivation is relatively new in Spain, dating back only to the mid-nineteenth century. Today Valencia lates are widely grown in the citrus fields of Arizona, California, Florida and Texas, as well as various parts of the southern hemisphere.

The navel orange gets its name from the small embryonic fruit growing inside it, making it look rather like a belly button. Despite this apparent fecundity, the navel orange can be propagated only by the use of cuttings. Seedless, navels have large, juicy segments, making them ideal for eating (though, personally, give me a blood orange any day). One of the most popular varieties is the Washington, also known as the Bahia, the region of Brazil from which it was introduced to America in the late nineteenth century.

The blood orange, so-called because of its blood-red flesh, is believed to have originated in Sicily, which certainly remains one of the major producing areas. Originally

RUBOR

García Gallén

VILLARREAL · ESPAÑA

too small to be popular, it has been bred to increase in size. Sanguinello is a particularly common variety, producing fine juice. Earlier in the season come the Moros, recalling the Moors who first brought oranges to Sicily. Tarocco is a mid-season variety with good flavor and a delicate flesh.

The bitter, or Seville, orange was the first orange to be cultivated by the Moors when they planted orange trees in their conquered lands, from Spain to Sicily. Even as late as the eighteenth century many cookbooks advocating the use of an orange in a savory dish intended that the cook use a bitter variety, although this is not explicitly stated.

Seville oranges have a short season early in the year. They are the best fruit for making marmalade but also have culinary uses far beyond this. It is worth noting that Seville oranges freeze well whole. I also fill an ice cube tray or two with their wonderful juice, so that I can use it in sauces all year round. The zest of Seville oranges is especially useful when dried. Other good—but less common—varieties of bitter orange are Bouquet de Fleurs and Chinotto.

OTHER CITRUS FRUITS

Mandarins owe their name to the English word for a Chinese official—it may well have been just such a man who first brought them to European shores at the beginning of the nineteenth century, much later than other citrus fruits. The similar tangerines also owe their name to geography, because they were shipped to Europe via the Moroccan port of Tangiers. Both make good eating but their juices are not robust enough for cooking, and their zest does not dry well. The same applies to satsumas.

A quick word on limes. Some readers might wonder why I have chosen not to include limes in the scope of this book. Limes are, of course, used right across the world in all kinds of dishes. But the fact remains that they originated, and still grow best, in a distinctly tropical climate. Believed to come from Malaysia, they do not grow successfully farther north, and as a result they have not earned themselves a place in the traditions of cooking around the Mediterranean—which is what *Oranges & Lemons* is all about.

COMMERCIAL PRESERVING OF ORANGES & LEMONS

In these days of long-distance transport, oranges and lemons are routinely picked underripe. When I visited an orange-packing factory near Valencia, I found that much of the fruit was still tinged with green and was put in a cool area until it had reached a full orange color. One consequence of this is that oranges can be difficult to peel; only if they are allowed to ripen on the tree will their skin come away easily.

At the packing factories oranges and lemons are picked over to remove damaged fruit, washed, then sprayed with wax that both preserves them and gives them an appealing shine. If you are using the zest in a recipe, I would always suggest choosing unwaxed fruit, so that you are not adding this wax to the dish (though it is meant to be unharmful). There is also rising demand for organic oranges and lemons. Aware of this, commercial producers are making efforts to reduce the chemicals used, but many of them still have a long way to go.

The modern consumer's obsession with appearance means that much of the fruit produced for supermarkets is rejected, destined either to stay in the local farmer's market or to be made into preserves. At the orange factory I visited as much as 30 percent of the fruit was deemed too unsightly for some supermarket chains.

When buying oranges and lemons, remember that it is not just appearance that counts: Those varieties of knobbly, misshapen lemons have the sweetest flavor; an orange does not have to be perfectly symmetrical to be juicy. And take time to smell the fruit and squeeze the zest—fresh fruit will give out a little oil.

USING THE RIGHT EQUIPMENT

All you really need for cooking with oranges and lemons is a sharp knife, a solid chopping board and a bowl to catch the juices. But two pieces of equipment will make your life much easier. One is a juicer—not necessarily an electric one but a simple affair for hand-squeezing. I favor the old-fashioned type where you press the halved fruit down on a rounded, ridged point and the juice is caught in the bottom part. The other essential item is a zester, the type with four small holes at the top. This clever little device allows you to peel strips of zest thinly and quickly. And if you are going to be doing any preserving, then mason jars of various sizes are always very handy.

SOUPS

Soups are fast food these days—as long as someone else has prepared them, that is. In my opinion, the best soups still result from a long, gentle simmer. Not that this should trouble the cook; just leave the pot to bubble away, filling the kitchen with delicious scents. But soups made in this way often need a final sharpener. Greek avgolémono is a classic example: adding eggs and lemon transforms a simple chicken broth.

That final squeeze of orange or lemon in a soup is not new. One of my favorite English cookbook writers of the seventeenth century, Sir Kennelm Digby, suggests finishing his "ordinary potage" with "juyce of Orange." In Morocco, where the food retains strong similarities to that of England in Digby's day, and before, soups of pulses and meats are still finished with lemon—as they are in the eastern Mediterranean.

There are also soups where the fruit is put in at the beginning. The addition of orange at the early stages of a carrot soup brings out the sweetness of the vegetable, and the Greeks cook their substantial fish soups with plenty of orange juice. If, occasionally, cooking a soup seems too much effort, try a fresh tomato and orange consommé.

Carrot, Cardamom, & Orange Soup (see page 18)

A'DDAS
Spiced lemon and lentil soup

Serves 4

4 large **scallions**

3 **garlic cloves**

¼ cup **olive oil**

1 heaping cup **green lentils**, preferably
those from Le Puy

1 teaspoon **ground cumin**

1 **stick cinnamon**

2 small **dried red chiles**

1 large **red potato**, peeled and cut
into ¾ in. cubes

2 quarts **water**

2 **lemons**

1 large handful **cilantro** leaves

Sea salt and freshly ground **black
pepper**

*The Lebanon is the original melting pot of the Mediterranean: It has seen many
cultures come and go, including that of the people of the sea, the Phoenicians, and
the Greeks, Romans, and Ottomans amongst others. Each brought their own
culinary traditions, which have been melded together by the inventive Lebanese to
create perhaps the most refined cuisine of the eastern Mediterranean (though the
Turks would undoubtedly dispute that claim).*

*Yet despite their elegant mezze tables, covered with tasty morsels to nibble, the
Lebanese also retain a tradition of hearty mountain foods, such as this lentil
soup. A'ddas is particularly popular during the Muslim month of Ramadan,
eaten at dusk to break the fast. Adding lemon brings out the flavor of the spices
and at the same time lifts this substantial soup.*

Roughly chop the scallions and finely chop 1 garlic clove. Heat half the
olive oil in a large saucepan and add the onions and chopped garlic.
Cook for 10 minutes, stirring occasionally, until the onion has softened.

Pour the lentils into the pot and add the cumin, cinnamon, chiles,
and black pepper. Stir the lentils well to coat with the oil. Add the potato
and water. Raise the heat to bring the water to a boil, then turn down to
a simmer, cover, and cook for 30 minutes. Add 1 teaspoon sea salt
halfway through the cooking time.

Squeeze the juice from 1 lemon and thinly slice the other one.
When the lentils are very tender, take the soup off the heat and add the
lemon juice and slices. Chop the cilantro roughly and add to the soup.
Let stand for 10 minutes.

Meanwhile, cut the remaining garlic into fine flakes. Heat the
remaining oil and fry the garlic flakes until lightly browned—take care
they do not burn or they will taste bitter. Drain on paper towels.

To serve, ladle the soup into bowls, making sure each has a slice of
lemon. Check seasoning and sprinkle with the garlic flakes.

CARROT, CARDAMOM, & ORANGE SOUP

Serves 4

1 lb **carrots**

2 tablespoons **unsalted butter**

2 **cardamom pods**

Good pinch of **saffron strands**

Good pinch of **sugar**

2 **garlic cloves**

1 piece **fresh ginger** about ¾ in.
  square, peeled and finely chopped

6 **dried apricots**, ready soaked,
  roughly chopped

Juice of 4 large **oranges**

5½ cups **water**

Sea salt and freshly ground **black
  pepper**

Carrots and oranges have a natural affinity. The Moroccans, for example, serve finely grated carrots mixed with fat, juicy segments of orange in a lightly spiced salad dressed with orange-flower water (see page 93). Orange added to a carrot soup brings out the natural sweetness of the vegetable without the soup becoming cloying. I also add a few dried apricots and fresh ginger, along with expensive saffron to lend its unique honeyed flavor, and cardamom pods for fragrance.

This recipe is based on a soup I was served in the mountains of the Hunza Valley in northern Pakistan, where the people grow the most exquisite apricots and dry them on the roofs of the houses. When I first ate the soup it was mixed with swollen grains of barley to add bulk, but I prefer the more refined version. It is particularly good served with flat Arabic bread that you have lightly toasted in the broiler. (Photograph on page 14)

Scrub the carrots well and chop roughly. Put them in a large saucepan with the butter, cardamom, saffron, pepper, sugar, whole garlic cloves, and ginger. Cook over a medium heat for 5 minutes, stirring regularly, until the spices have released their fragrance and the carrots are very lightly browned.

Add the apricots and orange juice, together with a generous shake of salt. Keep heating and, as soon as the orange juice comes to a boil, add the water. Bring back to a boil, turn down to a simmer, cover, and cook for 45 minutes.

Let cool for 10 minutes, then liquidize thoroughly. Check seasoning and reheat gently before serving.

HARIRA
Ramadan soup

This is another Ramadan soup, this time from the western side of the Mediterranean. Harira is the classic soup of the fasting month in Morocco and, like a'ddas (see page 16), has a base of spiced pulses, perked up with lemon juice and herbs. Instead of potato, vermicelli is used to provide bulk. Traditionally, the soup was finished with a thickening of fermented flour and water.

This is the fast-food version, Moroccan style, using canned or bottled stock, canned chickpeas, and canned tomatoes. It still needs to cook for an hour or so, but then four or more would be customary for the classic version, served at dusk each evening of Ramadan in the Djemaa el Fna marketplace in Marrakesh. As with a'ddas, this soup is a meal in itself, designed to satisfy the hunger of someone who has been fasting from sun-up to sundown.

Place the stock in a large pot and bring to a boil. Finely chop a handful each of cilantro and parsley leaves, and set aside. Tie the remaining herbs into a bunch, leaving the stalks on, and add to the stockpot.

Add the lentils, turmeric, cinnamon, ginger, cumin, 1 teaspoon black pepper, salt to taste, and olive oil to the pot. Simmer, covered, for 20 minutes, then add the chickpeas, tomatoes, vermicelli, and grated onion. Simmer for a further 20 minutes. Remove the tied bunch of herbs.

Check seasoning, remove from the heat, and add the lemon juice, the chopped cilantro and parsley, and the reserved tomato juice. Slice the lemon. Serve each bowl of soup with a slice of lemon dusted finely with ground cinnamon.

Serves 4

4½ pints **chicken** or **lamb stock**
1 large bunch **cilantro**
1 large bunch **fresh parsley**
⅔ cup **red lentils**
1 teaspoon **turmeric**
2 teaspoons **ground cinnamon**
1 teaspoon **ground ginger**
1 teaspoon **ground cumin**
3 tablespoons **olive oil**
16-oz can **chickpeas**, drained
16-oz can **plum tomatoes**, roughly
   chopped, reserving the juice
4 oz **vermicelli,** broken
1 large **Spanish onion**, grated
3–4 tablespoons freshly squeezed
   lemon juice
1 **lemon**
ground cinnamon, for dusting
Sea salt and freshly ground **black**
   pepper

AVGOLEMONO SOUPA
Chicken soup with eggs and lemon

A spoonful of this famous soup of Greece illustrates far more than words ever can how the juice of a lemon or two can transform a dish. Avgolémono (Greek for "eggs and lemon") is nothing more than chicken broth thickened with eggs beaten with fresh lemon juice, and yet its flavor is so delicate, so perfumed, and so refreshing that it is hard to believe it is produced by such a simple act in the kitchen.

Just one warning: This does merit chicken stock made with a bird rather than a cube. It's not exactly an effort—some chicken wings or a leftover carcass, water of course, perhaps an onion, a carrot or two, and a sprig of parsley, certainly a grind of pepper and a pinch of salt, and finally a splash of white wine or vermouth. Let the pot simmer for a couple of hours and there you are. It is worth it—and you can freeze the stock until you want to make soup.

Bring the stock to a boil. Rinse the rice thoroughly several times, then add to the boiling stock with the salt. Boil for 10 minutes or until the rice is cooked through.

Beat together the whole eggs, the egg yolk, and the lemon juice. Add 1 tablespoon hot stock to this mixture and whisk. Now take the soup off the heat and whisk in the egg-and-lemon mixture. Beat for 2 minutes, until you have a slightly thickened, creamy soup; do not bring the soup back to a boil or it will curdle. Sprinkle with the fresh dill and float a slice of lemon in each bowl before serving.

Serves 4

3¼ pints rich **chicken stock**

3 tablespoons **long-grain rice**, such as Basmati

Good pinch of **sea salt**

3 large **eggs** plus 1 **egg yolk**

½ cup **freshly squeezed lemon juice**

1 tablespoon finely chopped **fresh dill**

4 thin slices **lemon**

Note: For those concerned about the possible health risk, the eggs in this recipe are not cooked through fully.

KAKAVIA
Greek fish soup

Serves 6–8

2 large **Spanish onions**, finely chopped

½ cup **olive oil**

3 fat **garlic cloves**, quartered

2 large **red potatoes**, total weight about 1¼ lb, peeled and chopped into 1¼ in. chunks

2¼ lb ripe, flavorful **tomatoes**, quartered

3 **oranges**

¼ cup **freshly squeezed lemon juice**

1 heaping teaspoon **sea salt**

1 heaping teaspoon **paprika**

Good pinch of **saffron strands**

Several sprigs **fresh, flat-leaf parsley**

1 large sprig **fresh thyme**

11 oz small, prepared **squid**, the bodies cut across into several pieces, tentacles reserved (note: if using frozen, prepared squid, the tentacles may be tucked inside the body)

1 whole **silver mullet** (about 1 lb), head and tail removed and set aside

11 oz **tuna loin**

1¼ lb **mussels** in the shell

6 small fresh **sardines**, gutted and scaled (and heads removed if you are of a delicate nature)

1 **lemon**, cut into wedges, to serve

Fish soup is served all around the Mediterranean, but it is often claimed that the original is based on the classic Greek fisherman's soup, kakavia. More rough and ready than bouillabaisse, this is a soup defined by the day's catch, to be cooked on board ship—all the fish too small for market go in the pot. Plenty of fruity olive oil, some potatoes for bulk, garlic and onions for flavor, spices and tomatoes for color and sweetness—and the juice of oranges and lemons. I was once told that the fruit was used because it is easier to transport than drinking water. Use whatever fish you have to hand, but this combination is my favorite.

Put the onions, oil, and garlic in a large metal pot over a moderate heat. Cook for 10–15 minutes, stirring occasionally, then add the cubed potatoes. Cook for another 10 minutes, then add the quartered tomatoes. Cook for another 10 minutes, stirring occasionally.

Meanwhile, pare a couple of slivers of orange zest and squeeze the juice from the oranges. Now add to the cooking mixture the orange zest, the orange juice and lemon juice, the salt, paprika, saffron, about 2½ cups water, and the parsley and thyme. Bring to a simmer and add the squid and the head and tail of the mullet. Cover and simmer for a further 30 minutes, until both the potatoes and the squid are tender.

Meanwhile, cut the remaining mullet across the bone into several pieces. Cut the tuna into generous, bite-sized chunks. Debeard the mussels and scrub thoroughly, discarding any that are open.

When the potatoes are ready, remove the mullet head and tail (though a Greek fisherman certainly wouldn't bother). Slip the mullet pieces and the tuna into the broth and cook for 5 minutes before adding the sardines and the mussels. Cover and cook for another 3–4 minutes, until the mussels are open, discarding any that remain closed. Serve with lots of crusty bread and lemon wedges to squeeze into the soup.

SIR DIGBY'S NOURISHING BROTH
Herb soup with orange

Sir Kennelm Digby was a seventeenth-century British epicure and diplomat. The collection of notes and recipes he left form a fascinating portrait of his era's tastes and still appeal today, despite the fact that he seems to have poisoned his wife. He often uses oranges and lemons to finish a dish, and his enthusiasm for oranges marks him as a show-off, as they were much prized and very costly. For this recipe, he suggests a "gelly-broth of Mutton, Veal, joynt-bones of each, a Hen, and some bones (with a little meat upon them) of rosted Veal or Mutton, breaking the bones that the marrow may boil out." I just use chicken stock—from a bird, not a cube.

Bring the chicken stock to a boil and add the onion, peppercorns, clove, mace or nutmeg, half the parsley and chives, and all the thyme and oregano or marjoram. Simmer very gently for 1½ hours and then strain. The liquid will have acquired a light green hue.

To serve, reheat the stock and add the remaining parsley leaves and chives, very finely chopped. Simmer for 10 minutes, until the herbs have wilted. Meanwhile, lightly toast the bread and stir together the eggs and orange juice. Remove the soup from the heat, stir in the egg-and-orange juice mixture, top with the toast, and serve.

Serves 4

4½ pints **chicken stock**

1 large **white onion**, quartered

20 whole **black peppercorns**

1 **clove**

1 blade **mace** or pinch of **ground nutmeg**

1 large bunch **fresh parsley**

1 large bunch **fresh chives**

4 sprigs **fresh thyme**

4 sprigs **fresh oregano** or **marjoram**

8 thin slices **French bread**

2 **eggs**, beaten

Juice of 1 large **orange**

Note: For those concerned about the possible health risk, the eggs in this recipe are not cooked through fully.

The Museum of the Orange
Burriana, to the north of Valencia, lies at the heart of Spain's orange industry, so it is fitting that it is the home of the Museu de la Taronja. Housed in an art deco building, this extraordinary museum is the inspiration of Vicente Abad, a man who is passionate about the history of the orange industry. There is a marvelous collection of labels from orange crates (see pages 12–13), examples of flamboyant fashions worn by the womenfolk of the orange barons, and evocative sepia photos of orange harvests in the 1920s and 1930s.

CHILLED TOMATO & ORANGE CONSOMME

Serves 4

1 lb **fresh plum tomatoes**

9 oz **cherry tomatoes**

Juice of 3 large **oranges**

2 x 10 oz cans **concentrated beef consommé**

Generous dash iced **vodka**

Generous handful **fresh basil leaves,** torn into pieces

1 **orange**, to serve

There is a drink known as a bullshot, made simply from vodka and beef consommé. It has the effect of being both warming and restoring, although it is at its best served ice cold. This French soup has similar properties, for those days when you are feeling a little weak. The tomatoes and orange make sure you get plenty of vitamin C, so think of it as healthy as well (as long as you go easy with the vodka). And nothing could be simpler to make, which is necessary for hangover food. Perfect for New Year's Day.

Pour boiling water over the plum tomatoes and let stand for about 30 seconds. Peel the tomatoes, cut in half, and remove all the seeds. Chop the flesh very finely. Wash the cherry tomatoes and quarter.

Mix the orange juice into the beef consommé in a bowl and add the chopped plum tomato flesh and the quartered cherry tomatoes. Place the bowl in the freezer for at least 1 hour, until the liquid around the edge has just started to freeze. Just before serving, stir in the vodka and the basil leaves. Serve with quarters of orange to squeeze into the soup.

FISH

Many of the meals that have left the most indelible impression on me have involved fish on my plate, a glass of cool white wine at hand, shady citrus groves nearby—and the Mediterranean within sight.

It's pretty obvious that lemon goes with fish and shellfish. Baby goatfish, lightly coated in flour and deep-fried in olive oil; fresh oysters on the half shell; a whole sea bass lightly broiled and sprinkled with nothing more than salt. All these need a squeeze of sharpening juice. But this is lemon as the finishing touch, one that does not need much imagination. It is recipes where the lemon takes its place in a marinade or in an accompanying sauce that I have concentrated on here.

Orange and fish is a less obvious partnership, but a great one. Orange butter served on a broiled flat fish is a classic, and trout stuffed with orange slices before broiling is fantastic. Orange and tomato sauce is a favorite accompaniment to red mullet (a type of goatfish) in Provence and to tuna in Sicily. Use oranges as you would lemons; for example, with Dover sole serve orange quarters rather than the harsher lemon, which can overwhelm the delicate flavor of the fish, or squeeze a Seville orange over shrimp fried with lots of garlic and a splash of fino sherry.

Lemon-marinated Garlic Shrimp (see page 30)

KILIC SISTE TARATOR
Marinated swordfish kebabs with walnut sauce

Serves 4

FOR THE KEBABS

1 lb **swordfish steak**, cut into slices at least 1 in. thick

¼ cup **freshly squeezed lemon juice**

¼ cup **extra-virgin olive oil**

1 teaspoon **sweet paprika**

16 **fresh bay leaves**

Sea salt and freshly ground **black pepper**

Kebab skewers (soaked in water first if wooden, to prevent them from burning)

FOR THE TARATOR SAUCE

1 cup **walnuts**, shelled and peeled

3 **garlic cloves**

½ teaspoon **sea salt**

2 slices **white country bread**, crusts removed

⅔ cup **extra-virgin olive oil**

¼ cup **lemon juice**

TO SERVE

Flat bread

1 **lemon**, quartered

There's nothing like taking a boat trip to get you in the mood for lunch. And that's just what you do in Istanbul on the weekend, when the ferries crisscrossing the Bosphorus are packed with locals looking forward to a feast of fish, whether it be at one of the restaurants on Princes' Islands or those that line either side of the narrow strait leading to the Black Sea.

The Turks are masters of the kebab and they don't restrict their skill to the barbecuing of meat. Hefty chunks of swordfish, threaded onto skewers and interspersed with fresh bay leaves, are a favorite. The fish is first marinated in oil and lemon, which has the effect of part-cooking it, before being quickly grilled over charcoal. But the real secret to this dish is the tarator sauce served with the fish—an unctuous mixture of walnuts pounded with bread, garlic, oil, and lemon that was a favorite with the fat pashas of the Ottoman Empire.

Cut the swordfish into 1-in. cubes and place in an earthenware dish. Beat together the lemon juice and olive oil, and add the paprika and plenty of salt and pepper. Pour this mixture over the swordfish, turning the cubes to coat them, and set in a cool place to marinate for at least 4 hours, preferably overnight.

To make the tarator sauce, grind together the walnuts, garlic, and salt until you have a paste. Traditionally, this is done with a mortar amd pestle, which does achieve the best result, but the food processor is a very quick and easy alternative.

Soak the bread briefly in water and squeeze dry. Using the back of a wooden spoon, combine the walnut paste with the bread. Mix the olive oil with the lemon juice, and then slowly beat this emulsion into the walnut mixture until you have a smooth sauce.

Pour boiling water over the bay leaves, set aside for 1 hour, then drain. This softens the leaves and prevents them from burning.

When you are ready to cook the kebabs, have the charcoals just glowing or the broiler preheated. Thread 4 cubes of fish onto each skewer, interspersing them with the soaked bay leaves. Cook for 12–15 minutes, turning several times and basting frequently with the marinade. Serve with the tarator sauce, flat bread, and lemon quarters.

LEMON-MARINATED GARLIC SHRIMP

Serves 4 as an appetizer or as one of a selection of tapas

1 lb large **raw shrimp**, in their shells

3 small **dried red chiles**

2 **garlic cloves**, finely chopped

1 teaspoon **coarse sea salt**

½ cup **lemon juice**

¼ cup **extra-virgin olive oil**

One of the many things I love about Spain is that, however far you are from the coast, the seafood is of a quality and freshness that is rare in many other parts of the world. Mind you, these days Spain imports quite a bit of fish from elsewhere. Not the shrimp, however, which are still trawled off the Spanish coast in quantity, and can be appreciated at their very best served from the grill as a tapa, the small dishes Spaniards enjoy before the main meal.

The freshest shrimp need only a dusting of coarse sea salt and a squeeze of lemon juice before being thrown directly over the heat. I remember eating them this way in Jerez (the Andalusian town that gave its name to sherry), with a glass of chilled manzanilla that had its own salty tang. But those you buy will benefit from a brief dip in a garlicky mixture of lemon juice and oil before you cook them—preferably on the barbecue.

It is important to use raw shrimp for this dish—those pink ones precooked at sea are beyond redemption. (Photograph on page 26)

Wash the shrimp well, removing any eggs (roe) if necessary, and pat dry. Place in a china or earthenware bowl. Crumble the chiles and sprinkle over the shrimp, along with the chopped garlic and salt. Beat together the lemon juice and olive oil. Pour this mixture over the shrimp.

Let the shrimp marinate in the refrigerator for at least 4 hours, turning them once or twice.

When you are ready to cook, either get the barbecue coals glowing or heat a griddle or skillet, preferably a ridged one, over a high heat. Remove the shrimp from the marinade and grill them for 3–4 minutes on each side, depending on their size—they will turn pink when cooked. While they are cooking, baste them regularly with the marinade. In the last minute of cooking, pour the remaining marinade over the shrimp.

Serve very hot, with extra lemon wedges if you like.

TROUT IN ORANGE MARINADE

The first Italian cookbook I ever owned was one written by the doyenne of Italian culinary writing, Marcella Hazan, and it has long stood me in good stead. Marcella writes about the sort of food I knew as a child in Italy, good local home cooking. This recipe for trout that is first fried and then marinated in herb-scented olive oil, fruit juice, and vermouth is based on one of Marcella's and is a good example of her approach: simple, inexpensive ingredients made special. It is an inspired way of making farmed trout more exciting.

Wash the trout well inside and out and pat dry. You can, if you like, remove the head and tail—it certainly makes it easier to find a skillet in which both fish will lie flat, which is important. It is also best to use a non-stick pan.

Heat the oil in the skillet over a medium-high heat. Scatter the flour over a dry surface and carefully roll the fish in it, making sure the flesh is well-coated on both sides. When the oil is hot but not spitting, carefully slip in the fish and fry for 4 minutes on one side, until nicely browned. Turn over carefully and fry for a further 4 minutes. Lift the fish out with a slotted spoon and place in an earthenware or china dish in which they fit snugly (do not use metal, as it will taint the marinade).

Cut the zest of half the orange into thin strips, avoiding the pith. Squeeze the juice of the orange, and set juice and zest aside.

Return the skillet in which the fish cooked to a medium heat, keeping all the oil, and add the chopped onion. Fry for about 5 minutes, stirring regularly, until the onion is lightly golden.

Add the vermouth and the orange zest to the skillet with the onion and let the wine bubble for 30 seconds, stirring all the time. Now add the orange and lemon juices, bring back to a boil, and bubble for another 30 seconds. Add the bay leaves and chopped parsley, a good sprinkling of salt and a few generous grinds of black pepper, and then pour the hot marinade over the fish—it should just cover them.

Let the fish cool at room temperature for at least 4 hours before transferring the dish to the refrigerator overnight. Serve the next day as an antipasto with lots of bread.

Serves 4 as an appetizer or antipasto

2 medium-sized **rainbow trout**, about 12 oz each

6 tablespoons **extra-virgin olive oil**

¼ cup **all-purpose flour**

1 large **orange**

1 small **onion**, finely chopped

¾ cup **Italian white vermouth**

¼ cup **freshly squeezed lemon juice**

2 **fresh bay leaves**

1 tablespoon chopped **fresh, flat-leaf parsley**

Sea salt and freshly ground **black pepper**

GOATFISH PROVENCAL

Serves 4 as an appetizer or light
main course

4 small **goatfish**

1 lb 10 oz **fresh plum tomatoes**

½ cup **extra-virgin olive oil**

2 **garlic cloves**, finely chopped

2 **oranges**: 1 for juice, 1 for zest and
slicing

Good bunch of **fresh basil leaves**,
torn into pieces

Flour

16 small **black olives**, preferably
preserved with orange peel
(seepage 130)

Sea salt and freshly ground **black**
pepper

Provençal cooks often flavor their tomato sauces with a little orange, but rarely to more effect than in this dish. In Provence, red mullet is the fish of choice for this recipe, but its close relative the goatfish tastes just as good bathed in fresh tomato sauce. This dish has to me all my favorite flavors of the sunny south—fresh fish, olive oil, tomatoes, herbs, and tiny black olives, all imbued with a hint of orange perfume. The Mediterranean on a plate.

Scale and gut the fish, if the fishseller has not already done so, leaving in the liver if you like (this is traditional in Provence to give a slight gaminess to the fish). Pour boiling water over the tomatoes and let stand for about 30 seconds. Peel, cut in half, remove all the seeds, and chop the flesh. Preheat the oven to 350°F.

Heat half the olive oil in a heavy-based skillet over a medium heat. Add the garlic and, as soon as it begins to sizzle, the chopped tomatoes, the juice of 1 orange, several strips of orange zest, and a good pinch of salt. Simmer uncovered for 12–15 minutes, stirring occasionally to help the tomatoes break down, until you have a thick tomato sauce. Remove from the heat and add half the basil.

Season the flour well and lightly dust over both sides of the fish. Heat the remaining oil over a high heat in a non-stick skillet in which all the fish will lie flat. When the oil is very hot, add the fish and fry for 2 minutes on each side. Remove the fish carefully with a slotted spoon.

Place the fish in an earthenware dish in which they lie flat and dot with the tomato sauce. Cut the remaining orange into slices. Sprinkle the olives around the fish and arrange the orange slices on top. Place in the preheated oven and bake for 15 minutes. Serve very hot straight from the dish, sprinkled with the remaining torn basil.

SAMAK CHERMOULA
Grilled fish with lemon and herb marinade

Serves 4

2 **sea bass** or **silver mullet**, each about
    1½ lb, gutted and scaled

2 **garlic cloves**, finely chopped

½ teaspoon **ground cumin**

2 teaspoons **paprika**

¼ teaspoon **cayenne pepper**

2 tablespoons finely chopped **cilantro**

2 tablespoons finely chopped
    fresh, flat-leaf parsley

1 tablespoon finely chopped
    celery leaves

¼ cup **freshly squeezed lemon juice**

¼ cup **extra-virgin olive oil**

½ **preserved lemon**, finely chopped,
    optional (see page 120)

Sea salt

Chermoula is one of the gifts of Moroccan cooking. A simple marinade of spices, herbs, oil and lemon, it transforms a fish destined for the barbecue, the oven, or the tagine, the conical cooking pot that is such a feature of Moroccan kitchen life. Variants of chermoula are prepared all over the country, using different mixes of spices and herbs, and various kinds of fish, but one principle remains constant— the fish must be left to absorb the marinade before it is cooked. The end result is peculiarly succulent. The preserved lemon is not essential, but it does add a uniquely Moroccan flavor.

Make several deep slashes across the flesh on each side of the fish, cutting right down to the bone.

To make the chermoula marinade, mix together all the remaining ingredients except the preserved lemon. The consistency should be almost that of a paste—in Morocco this is achieved with a mortar and pestle, but use a food processor if you prefer. Be careful, however, that the herbs do not break down into a slimy mush. When the chermoula is ready, stir in the preserved lemon, if you are using it.

Spread the chermoula all over the fish, making sure plenty gets down into the slashes. Marinate for 2–3 hours.

To cook the fish, preheat the broiler or, better still, get the barbecue coals glowing. Broil or grill the fish close to the heat for about 8–10 minutes on each side, until the flesh lifts away easily from the bone. Serve with bread, a crisp green salad, and quarters of lemon.

You can also bake this dish, wrapping the fish in foil.

MARINATED SQUID WITH BEAN SALAD

There are two ways to cook squid: very quickly or very slowly. To achieve the first method most successfully, you need to marinate the squid, and citric juice is just perfect here, helping to soften and part-cook the squid before its brief flash on a griddle. Squid is delicious but rich. I got the idea of mixing it with beans from the classic Italian tuna and bean salad, and now this dish is a firm favorite.

Remove the tentacles. Cut the bodies of the squid down one side of the tube so that the flesh lies flat. (Note: the tentacles may be tucked inside the body, so don't slice these too, by mistake; remove them first). With a sharp knife, score the body across several times diagonally. Lay the bodies and tentacles in a dish and add the orange juice and half the lemon juice. Season well. Peel and cut the garlic into flakes, crumble the chiles, and sprinkle both over the squid. Marinate for about 1 hour.

Meanwhile, cook the beans. Bring a large suacepan of water to a boil; do not add salt, which toughens the beans. Add the beans and simmer for about 45 minutes, until tender. If using canned beans, drain, then heat gently in water until warm. Drain the beans and put into a wide, fairly deep serving dish. Stir in the olive oil, remaining lemon juice, and plenty of seasoning while the beans are hot. Add the onion, cherry tomatoes, and basil leaves.

When you are ready to cook the marinated squid, heat up a lightly oiled, ridged griddle or skillet until very hot. (You can cook this on a non-ridged griddle or skillet, but you won't achieve an attractive striped finish.) Now remove the squid from the marinade, shaking off any excess. Put the tentacles on the griddle first and cook for 1 minute; then add the bodies and cook them for no more than 1 minute on each side. Arrange the hot squid over the beans. Now pour the marinade, including the garlic flakes, onto the griddle and cook for 1 minute, until the marinade bubbles up. Pour this too over the beans and squid and serve with lots of bread. In the unlikely event that there are any leftovers, this salad is also good cold.

Serves 4

4 prepared **squid**, with tentacles, about 1 lb total cleaned weight

Juice of 1 large **orange**

½ cup **freshly squeezed lemon juice**

1 large **garlic clove**

2 small **dried red chiles**

1 lb **fresh borlotti or cranberry beans**

3 tablespoons **extra-virgin olive oil**

1 small **red onion,** finely chopped

8 **cherry tomatoes**, roughly chopped

1 handful **fresh basil leaves,** torn into pieces

Sea salt and freshly ground **black pepper**

COD CEVICHE

The most famous fish dish of Central and South America, ceviche gains its name from escabeche, *the Portuguese and Spanish method of marinating and cooking fish and meat in vinegar in order to preserve it. The vinegar was replaced by lemon or lime juice and somewhere along the line the cooking was forgotten, leaving the fish to be cured in the acid juices. Ceviche today is just as popular in Portugal, where it is often made with cod, mixed with lemon juice and plenty of cilantro.*

Cut the fish into bite-sized pieces. Place it in a china or earthenware container into which it will just fit. Scatter the chopped chiles over it. Add the whole peppercorns and the salt, and stir well. Sprinkle with the chopped red onion. Now pour on the lemon juice—there should be just enough to cover the fish.

Refrigerate for 4 hours, stirring several times. At the end of this time the fish should have turned translucent—it will, in effect, have been "cooked" in the citric juices. Sprinkle with the fresh cilantro leaves just before serving. A tomato and onion salad and some crusty bread are excellent accompaniments to this dish.

Serves 4

14 oz boneless, skinless **cod**

1 **mild, long green chile**, seeded and finely chopped

1 **mild, long red chile**, seeded and finely chopped

10 **black peppercorns**

½ teaspoon **sea salt**

½ **red onion**, finely chopped

¾–1 cup **freshly squeezed lemon juice**

2 handfuls **fresh cilantro leaves**, chopped

TUNA WITH SEVILLE ORANGE SAUCE

Serves 4

2 **Seville oranges**

1 large **sweet orange**

¼ cup **extra-virgin olive oil**

4 thick-cut **tuna steaks**

1 large **Spanish onion**

5 sprigs **fresh, flat-leaf parsley**

2 sticks **celery**, preferably with
   leaves attached

2 cups canned Italian **plum tomatoes**

1 teaspoon **red wine vinegar**

½ teaspoon **sugar**

Sea salt and freshly ground **black
   pepper**

Each year in the month of June an extraordinary ritual takes place in the seas surrounding Favignana, off Trapani on the west coast of Sicily. This is the time of the tuna migration, and the fish are killed according to traditions brought by Moorish invaders more than a thousand years ago. As the captain chants Arabic songs and bangs out a rhythm on his drum, a vast net is slowly hauled in by hand from a flotilla of boats, trapping the tuna until the sea becomes a mass of thrashing fish. When the kill finally commences, the sea turns red.

Once the tuna was canned, but today the canneries lie empty, for there are far fewer fish and their value has rocketed, so that few are eaten in Sicily; the very best are flown directly to Japan. For eating those left behind, this recipe is a favorite treatment, using the bitter oranges that the Moors introduced to Sicily.

Squeeze the juice from the oranges, reserving the skin of half a Seville orange for later use. Mix the juice with half the olive oil and pour over the tuna steaks. Season well with black pepper and set aside to marinate for at least 2 hours, turning halfway through.

To make the sauce, peel and finely chop the onion. Also chop the parsley, including the stalks, and the celery, including the leaves. Heat the remaining oil in a heavy-based skillet over a medium-low heat and add the onions, celery, and parsley. Cook gently for 10 minutes, stirring regularly, until the onion is soft.

Cut off a strip of the Seville orange peel, making sure you avoid all pith, and cut the zest into 12 very thin slivers. Set aside.

Now add to the sauce the tomatoes, 1 tablespoon water, the vinegar, sugar, and a good pinch of salt. Simmer for 15 minutes and strain. Place the strained tomato sauce in a heavy-based saucepan with most of the orange zest (reserve some for a garnish) and strain the marinade into it. Reheat gently, stirring regularly. Remove the pot from the heat and check the seasoning.

To cook the fish, place a lightly greased griddle over a medium-high heat or broil in a ridged pan to get the attractive stripes. Grill or broil the tuna for 3–5 minutes on each side, depending on the thickness of the steaks—it should still be pink in the middle.

Serve the tuna in a pool of sauce, garnished with a little zest.

SAMAK TARATOOR
Broiled fish with sesame seed sauce

Serves 4

2 **fish**, each about 1½ lb, scaled and
  gutted (silver mullet, sea bass, and
  sea bream are good choices)

Extra-virgin olive oil

4 **garlic cloves**, finely chopped

3 tablespoons chopped **fresh,
  flat-leaf parsley**

3 tablespoons chopped **fresh cilantro**

¾ cup **freshly squeezed lemon juice**

1 cup **light tahini sauce**

Sea salt

One of the aspects of eating in the Lebanon of which I am especially fond is the restaurateurs' habit of displaying that day's catch in a chilled cabinet for customers' viewing—much more effective than looking over a printed menu.

Whatever the fish and however it is cooked, it is likely to be served with a pitcher of the sesame seed and lemon sauce known as taratoor, similar to the Turkish version in name only (see page 28). Pale gold in color and smooth in consistency, Lebanese taratoor is also incredibly easy to make. And, as the people of the Lebanon know so well, its nutty, sharp flavor enhances a fish no end. In fact, I find it positively addictive.

Wash the fish thoroughly. Using a sharp knife, cut 4 deep slashes across the flesh, right down to the bone, on each side. Rub in plenty of olive oil and salt and set aside for 1 hour.

Crush the garlic with some salt. Mix the parsley with the cilantro, the crushed garlic, ¼ cup lemon juice, and 2 tablespoons olive oil. Stuff this mixture into the cavity of the fish.

Drain the oil off the tahini sauce. Beat ¼ cup water into the sauce—surprisingly, this will thicken it. Then add the rest of the lemon juice—this will thin it. And there you have your taratoor sauce.

Preheat the broiler and broil the fish for 8–10 minutes on each side, until you can see clearly through to the bone and the skin is nicely blackened. Better still, cook the fish over charcoal. Serve the fish hot, with the taratoor sauce on the side.

MUSSEL & LEMON SALAD

I love mussels. I spent several formative childhood years living in Brussels and at lunch on Sundays would regularly tuck into that Belgian classic—a vast pot of the shellfish swimming in white wine, with a plate of fries, and, of course, a bowl of mayonnaise on the side. This is cold weather food, to be eaten in the cozy warmth of the restaurant while the wind swirls (or, in Brussels, rain pours down) outside.

But there is another way with mussels, more suited to those sunny evenings in the Mediterranean that most of us can only dream of. Marinated in a simple mixture of olive oil, lemon juice, and garlic, and then sprinkled with handfuls of flat-leaf parsley, they make an exquisite salad. It is also beautiful to look at, the shiny blue-black of the mussel shells contrasting with the vivid lemon. Imagine yourself in a Greek taverna beside the sea as you tuck in.
(Photograph on opening pages of book)

Serves 4

4½ lb **fresh mussels** in their shells

3 fat **garlic cloves**

½ teaspoon **sea salt**

½ cup **freshly squeezed lemon juice**

1 cup **extra-virgin olive oil**

2 large handfuls of **fresh, flat-leaf parsley**, leaves only

2 **lemons**, thinly sliced

Scrub the mussels thoroughly and debeard them (that is, remove the little strands sticking out of one side). Discard any mussels that have a cracked shell or do not close when tapped. Rinse well for several minutes under cold running water.

Using a mortar and pestle, crush the garlic cloves with the salt. Add the lemon juice and then slowly beat in the olive oil.

Place a saucepan large enough to contain all the mussels over a medium heat. Add 1 cup cold water and bring to a boil. Add the mussels and cover the pot. Cook for 5–6 minutes, stirring once and replacing the lid, until all the mussels have opened. Discard any that do not open.

Drain the mussels and place them in a large, wide bowl, preferably earthenware. Pour the garlic, lemon, and oil mixture over them. Roughly chop the flat-leaf parsley and sprinkle over the mussels. Place thin slices of lemon and delicate slivers of zest, if wanted, on the surface. Let cool before serving with crusty bread and perhaps a green salad.

SCALLOPS IN ORANGE SAUCE

Serves 4

3 **oranges** (Valencia lates are
   especially good for this recipe)

¾ cup **dry white wine**

1 teaspoonful **pastis** (e.g. Ricard)

Generous pinch of **sugar**

Pinch of **sea salt** and freshly ground
   black pepper

Generous pinch of **saffron strands**

2 **zucchini**

12 oz **scallops**, including corals
   where possible

¼ cup **unsalted butter**, chilled

The scallop is a gentle creature, and one that needs brief but fierce treatment. A piping hot broiler or a skillet of sizzling butter is the place to cook it—and as briefly as possible. Its sweet meat deserves a subtle sauce such as this one, based on orange juice and monter au beurre *in good French chef's fashion (this secret of a knob or two of cold butter to bring together a sauce is a cheffy favorite). The scallop corals look gorgeous against the delicate orange sauce and the vivid green zucchini. This, for once, is a restaurant dish that is easy to prepare* chez vous.

Squeeze the juice from the oranges. Place the juice, the wine, pastis, sugar, and salt in a heavy-based saucepan over a high heat. Bring to a boil. After the liquid has boiled for about 1 minute, lower the heat to medium and add the saffron strands. Let the liquid continue to bubble, uncovered, until it has reduced by just under half and acquired a slightly sticky quality. This will take 5–6 minutes; stir occasionally during this time. Remove from the heat.

Grate the zucchini. Bring a saucepan of salted water to a boil and blanch the zucchini for 30 seconds, then refresh immediately in cold water. Drain, gently squeezing the strands of zucchini to remove any excess moisture, and set aside.

Wash the scallops thoroughly. Choose a heavy-based skillet and add half the butter. Place over a medium-high heat and, when the butter has just started to fizz, add the scallops. Cook quickly for 2–3 minutes, according to size, turning several times. Take the skillet off the heat and remove the cooked scallops.

Now return the skillet to the heat and pour in the orange sauce. Bring back to a boil for about 1 minute while you cut the remaining butter into cubes. Quickly whisk the butter into the sauce and, as soon as the cubes have melted, add the scallops. Stir around once to coat the scallops and then add the zucchini strips and stir again. Remove from the heat immediately, add a grind of black pepper if liked, and serve without delay.

MEAT

A well-traveled friend recently described to me the culinary revelation he experienced in Florence when he ate a T-bone steak over which the waiter had squeezed half a lemon. "I really couldn't see the point of it—until I took a mouthful of the meat," he explained. My own moment of discovery was in Egypt, when I was served broiled chicken with just cumin seeds, coarse salt, and lots of lemon quarters. The succulence of the chicken was perfectly offset by the sharpness of the lemon juice. And, of course, the Spaniards know what they are doing when they put half an orange beside a pork chop.

These are examples of oranges and lemons as condiments, but these versatile fruits can benefit a meat dish at every stage of preparation and cooking. It may be the juice in the initial marinade; it could simply be half an orange popped inside a duck, or a lemon in a chicken for roasting. There is the swirl of citric juice to finish a butter sauce; the strips of preserved lemon for a Moroccan chicken tagine; the sliver of dried orange peel with daube of beef. All are subtle, but vital. And if I can't imagine a barbecue without oranges and lemons, I also use them in my winter stews.

Veal Scallops in Lemon Sauce (see page 48)

PATO SEVILLANA
Duck with olives and orange

Serves 4

4 **duck breasts**

½ teaspoon **sea salt**

1 teaspoon **sugar**

3 tablespoons **extra-virgin olive oil**

1 **white onion**, finely chopped

1 large **carrot**, finely chopped

½ head **celery**, including leaves,
    finely chopped

1 fat **garlic clove**, finely
    chopped

¾ cup **fino sherry**

Juice of 2 **Seville oranges**

1 large **orange**, cut into half-moon
    slices, including the peel

⅔ cup **cracked green olives**

2 small **dried red chiles**

1 large handful **fresh, flat-leaf
    parsley**, finely chopped

The first orange introduced to Spain in the eighth century by the Moors was the bitter orange, which later took its name from Seville. If you visit that glorious city today, you will still find orange trees in the court of the Moorish Alcazar Palace.

In their city Seville oranges grow so plentifully that they are left to drop from the trees. Elsewhere they still remain highly prized, due to their short season. And they are not just used for marmelada, *the conserve that gave its name to our orange marmalade, but also find their way into a variety of savory dishes; this is the Spanish way of combining them with duck.*

Slash the duck breasts several times across on the fat side until you just reach the pink flesh. Rub the salt and the sugar into the fat. Set aside for at least 1 hour.

Heat the oil in a heavy-based skillet over a medium heat. Add the onion, carrot, celery (including leaves), and garlic. Cook for about 20 minutes, stirring occasionally, until all the vegetables are tender. This stage can be done in advance.

When you are nearly ready to eat, preheat the broiler. Place a metal broiler pan in the broiler for 10 minutes. When the pan is hot, add the duck breasts, fat side up. Cook for 15 minutes, until the fat side is nicely browned (be careful the fat does not burn—if it looks like doing so, lower the broiler pan slightly). Remove the duck and let rest for 10 minutes.

While the duck is cooking, reheat the vegetables over a medium-high heat. When they are hot, pour in the fino sherry and cook for 2 minutes, allowing the liquid to bubble away. Now add the juice of the Seville oranges, the slices of orange, the olives, dried red chiles, and parsley. Cook for another 5 minutes, until the orange slices have softened and the orange juice reduced.

Taste the sauce—you may need to add a little sugar or salt, depending on the oranges and the olives. Cut the duck across into slices—the meat should be rosy. Arrange the vegetables and slices of orange across a serving plate, lay the duck on top, and serve. Rice flavored with saffron is a good accompaniment.

SCALLOPINE DI VITELLO AL LIMONE
Veal scallops in lemon sauce

Serves 2

(Best made for 2; if cooking for more,
* you have to fry the veal in 2 batches)*

2 large, thin **veal scallops**, each
    about 3–3½ oz

Flour

¼ cup **butter**

1 tablespoon **olive oil**

¼ cup **freshly squeezed lemon juice**

½ **lemon**, cut into 4 thin slices

2 tablespoons finely chopped **fresh,**
    flat-leaf parsley, leaves only

Sea salt and freshly ground **black**
    pepper

"Keep it simple" should, in my opinion, be the mantra for all cooks. This dish from northern Italy demonstrates the point admirably. To follow the rule, you must shop carefully, for simple cooking demands good ingredients. The veal should be from a calf reared in humane conditions. You need scallops cut against the grain and bashed flat, preferably by a butcher. They cannot be too thin. A good knob of butter, a little seasoning, some parsley and lemon juice, and there you are: fast food at its best. (Photograph on page 44)

Beat the veal scallops as flat as possible, using either a wooden rolling pin or spoon. Lightly sprinkle flour over a work surface or chopping board and season well. Preheat the oven to 300°F and place a serving dish inside to warm.

Melt half the butter with the oil in a heavy-based skillet over a medium heat. Turn the veal scallops in the seasoned flour, shaking off any excess. When the fat starts to fizz, raise the heat to medium-high and add the veal scallops. Provided they are beaten flat enough, they should take no more than 1 minute to cook on each side.

When they are lightly browned, take the scallops out of the skillet and transfer to the heated serving dish in the oven. Return the skillet to a medium heat and add the lemon juice to it, scraping well to stir in any residue. Add the lemon slices and the parsley, then quickly stir in the remaining butter. Stir until the butter has melted.

Return the cooked scallops to the skillet and turn to coat with the sauce. Arrange the veal scallops on the serving dish, pour the sauce over them, and serve immediately.

COLD CHICKEN WITH LEMON & HERBS

John Evelyn, a well-known English diarist of the 1600s, wrote an entire book on salads. "A Salet," he wrote, "is a Particular Composition of certain crude and fresh Herbes, such as usually are, or may be eaten, with some Acetuous Juice, Oyle, salt etc. to give them grateful gust and vehicle. In the composition of a Salet, every plant should come in to bear its part, without being overpowered by some herb of stronger taste . . . but fall into their place like the notes in music."

For those of us who associate the use of arugula, raddichio, baby spinach, and fresh herbs in salads with the late-twentieth century, it may be a surprise to learn that such ingredients were in common use so long ago, alongside edible flowers such as borage and nasturtium. And, as a final touch, such salads were decorated with thin slices of "citron or limon."

Shred the chicken meat. Quarter the lettuces. Arrange two quarters of lettuce on each plate, surrounded by the watercress, arugula, and sorrel. Sprinkle with the cooked chicken, parsley, tarragon, and oregano. To make the dressing, mix the vinegar and mustard with plenty of salt and pepper. Beat in the olive oil until well amalgamated, and then pour the dressing over the salad. Garnish with the slices of lemon.

Serves 4

1 small **skinless chicken breast**, cooked

2 **baby romaine lettuces**

1 large handful **watercress**

1 large handful **arugula leaves**

1 large handful **sorrel leaves**

1 tablespoon chopped **fresh, flat-leaf parsley**

1 tablespoon chopped **fresh tarragon**

¼ teaspoon **dried oregano**

2 tablespoons **white wine vinegar**

1 teaspoon **Dijon mustard**

½ cup **extra-virgin olive oil**

Sea salt and freshly ground black pepper

1 **lemon**, thinly sliced, to garnish

Menton's lemon festival

French legend has it that Eve stole a lemon before she and Adam were expelled from the Garden of Eden, and when they found their new paradise—on the Riviera, at Menton—they planted the fruit. For many centuries Menton lived from its citrus fruit industry. Today the industry has declined, with only 11 full-time fruit-growers still producing lemons locally, but Menton continues to celebrate its Fête du Citron in spectacular style. Started in 1876, the February festival has grown into a major affair, with oranges and lemons being used to garland floats and create sculptures ranging from tortoises to airplanes. Meanwhile, the Town Council is encouraging the replanting of Menton's once-famed groves.

LAMB KEBABS WITH TAHINI & ORANGE SAUCE

I first encountered this sauce served with the Lebanese favorite, kibbeh—an artful construction of lamb mixed with bulgur wheat and encasing yet more lamb flavored with spice. Kibbeh is delicious but tricky to make. The sauce, on the other hand, couldn't be simpler and is just as good an accompaniment to broiled chunks of lamb. I place all of it in a pocket of pita bread, with some green leaves, to make a classy sandwich. If Seville oranges are out of season, simply replace them with lemons.

Squeeze the juice of the Seville oranges, the clementines, and 1 sweet orange, and mix together. Beat ¼ cup juice with the olive oil. Pour this over the meat and marinate for several hours, stirring occasionally.

Drain the oil from the surface of the tahini, then beat the tahini and remaining fruit juice together to make the orange sauce.

Season the meat well, thread onto skewers and cook either over charcoal or in a hot broiler for 3–4 minutes on each side, until tender, basting with the marinade while the meat is cooking.

Meanwhile, warm the pita bread. Make a pocket on one side and spread in some of the orange sauce and a handful of arugula. Add the meat, pour a little more sauce over it, and serve with quarters of the remaining orange.

Serves 4

2 **Seville oranges**

2 **clementines**

2 large, **sweet oranges**

2 tablespoons **olive oil**

1¼ lb **leg** or **shoulder of lamb**, cut into bite-sized pieces

1 cup **light tahini sauce**

4 pieces **pita bread**

4 handfuls **arugula**

Sea salt and freshly ground **black pepper**

PECHUGAS DE POLLO EN SALSA DE NARANJAS
Chicken breasts in orange sauce

Serves 4

4 small **boneless, skinless chicken breasts**

¼ cup **unsalted butter**

1 tablespoon **olive oil**

Juice of 1 **Seville orange**

Juice of 2 large **sweet oranges**

1 tablespoon **pine nuts**, lightly toasted

1 tablespoon finely chopped **fresh mint**

Sea salt and freshly ground **black pepper**

This recipe comes from Valencia, the city known to the Spanish as the queen of oranges. It was Moorish invaders who first introduced oranges to Spain (albeit the bitter orange, which we know as Seville) and there are other traces of their centuries of occupation in this recipe. Find a savory dish with nuts in it and you can generally trace it to an ancient origin; and the use of mint is a very Moorish touch.

You don't need to restrict this simple recipe to the short Seville orange season—just substitute the juice of a lemon.

Place the chicken breasts between 2 sheets of plastic wrap and, using a rolling pin or the back of a wooden spoon, bang them to flatten them. Remove the plastic wrap and cut each breast in half across. Season the chicken breasts well. Preheat the oven to 300°F, and place a dish for serving the chicken inside.

Choose a heavy-based skillet in which all the breasts will fit, place it over a medium heat, and add half the butter and the oil. Cut the remaining butter into cubes and keep chilled. When the butter in the skillet is fizzing, add the chicken and fry for 3–4 minutes on each side, until lightly browned and cooked through (cut into a piece to check).

Transfer the chicken to the serving dish in the oven. Add all the orange juice to the skillet and raise the heat to high. Bubble the orange juice until it thickens slightly. Season the sauce, then quickly whisk in the cubes of chilled butter. Return the chicken breasts to the sauce, turning them once to coat, then pour the chicken and sauce onto the serving dish. Sprinkle with the pine nuts and mint and serve immediately.

ARNI FRIKASE AVGOLEMONO
Lamb fricassee with egg and lemon sauce

The Greeks don't use an egg-and-lemon mixture only to thicken soup (see
page 21). In spring, when the first lambs are slaughtered, the same mixture
finds its way into a delicate fricassee of meat with scallions and romaine lettuce.
Traditionally, the meat would be from very young animals and cooked on the
bone, but for our slightly more mature beasts, the tender fillet is a better choice.

Chop the lamb across into rounds about 1-in. thick, trimming off any fat.
Roughly chop the scallions, including the green part. Remove the heart
of the lettuce, discarding the outer leaves and the base. Wash the heart
well and chop across into strips roughly ¾ in. wide.

Heat the oil in a large skillet over a medium heat. Add the scallions
and lamb and fry for 3–4 minutes, turning the meat regularly, until it is
browned all over. Now add the stock, bring rapidly to a boil, and then
lower the heat to a simmer. Add the strips of lettuce and seasoning to
taste (if you are using a stock cube, go easy on the salt), and cook,
uncovered, for 5 minutes.

Meanwhile, beat the egg yolks with the lemon juice. Remove the
skillet from the heat and pour in the egg-and-lemon mixture, stirring all
the time. Place the skillet back on the heat at the lowest possible setting.
Cook for just 1 minute, still stirring, until the sauce thickens slightly—do
not let the sauce boil or it will curdle. Remove the skillet from the heat,
stir in the dill, check the seasoning, and serve with plain boiled rice.

Serves 4

1 lb boneless **neck of lamb**
2 bunches small **scallions**
1 large **romaine lettuce**
3 tablespoons **olive oil**
1 cup light **lamb stock**
3 large **egg yolks**
½ cup **freshly squeezed lemon juice**
1 tablespoon chopped **fresh dill**
Sea salt and freshly ground **black**
    pepper

LEMON-MARINATED CHICKEN WINGS

Serves 4

8 **chicken wings**

4 **garlic cloves**

1 teaspoon **sea salt**

¼ teaspoon **cayenne pepper**

¼ teaspoon freshly-ground **black
  pepper**

½ cup **freshly squeezed lemon juice**

¼ cup **extra-virgin olive oil**

4 sprigs **fresh thyme**

1 **lemon**, quartered, to serve

*Few of the dishes in an array of Lebanese mezze have escaped a brush with the
lemon. First there are the dips, hummus and moutabal—the purées of chickpeas
and charcoal-broiled eggplants, sharp with lemon juice and thick with olive oil.
There will always be tabbouleh (see page 79), green herbs flecked with bulgur
wheat and dressed with more lemon juice than oil, as is the crisp salad of bread,
purslane, tomatoes, and sumac seeds known as fattoush (see page 85). Then come
the hot dishes: perhaps sambousik (little pastries filled with ground lamb and pine
nuts), small, spicy Armenian sausages, or broiled köfte (lamb meatballs), with
quarters of lemon to squeeze over them.*

*My absolute favorite are the chicken wings, marinated in lemon juice, salt,
garlic, and olive oil, and cooked over charcoal until they are sweet and sticky,
slightly charred in patches, the flesh falling off the bones. They demand to be eaten
immediately. Serve with fattoush, as shown in the photograph, for a complete meal.*

Wipe the chicken wings and place in an earthenware bowl. Crush the
garlic with the salt, then add the cayenne and black peppers. Beat in the
lemon juice and olive oil. Add the leaves from the sprigs of thyme and
then pour the marinade over the chicken wings, turning well to coat
them in the mixture. Marinate for about 1 hour, turning once or twice.

Preheat a flat metal baking sheet in the broiler until it is very hot
(or, better still, cook the wings over the barbecue). Place the wings on
the baking sheet and cook for 20–25 minutes, turning once or twice and
basting frequently with the marinade until it is all used up and the wings
are lightly charred in places. Serve very hot with lemon quarters.

DUCK WITH BIGARADE SAUCE

Serves 4

1 large **sweet orange**

2 **Seville oranges**

2 **ducks**

Generous pinch of **sugar**

1 cup **rich stock**, preferably made
    from the giblets of the duck

1 cup **ruby port**

1 sprig **fresh thyme**

Sea salt and freshly ground **black
    peppe**r

"Bigarade" is the French name for the bitter or Seville orange and it is the use of this tart fruit that distinguishes the classic French version of duck à l'orange from others. Not that there is anything wrong with the others—providing that the sauce is not too sweet or cloying, it is one of my favorite dishes. Even easier and almost as effective is simply to squeeze the juice of an orange over a duck before roasting it with the orange zest firmly ensconced in its cavity. But bigarade is the ultimate in orange sauces for duck and not to be missed when Seville oranges are in season.

Preheat the oven to 400°F. Place half the sweet orange inside the cavity of each duck, season the skin generously, and place on a rack in a roasting pan (to catch all of the ducks' copious fat). Roast for 1 hour, basting several times with the fat.

While the ducks cook, prepare the sauce. Peel the zest of 1 Seville orange and cut it into thin strips. Extract the juice from both Seville oranges. Bring a small saucepan of water to a boil and blanch the zest for 1 minute, then drain well. Add the blanched zest, all the orange juice, the sugar, stock, and port to a small saucepan, together with the sprig of thyme. Bring to a boil, lower the heat, and simmer for 10–15 minutes, until nicely reduced.

Before serving, remove the thyme from the sauce and taste to check the balance of sweet and sour. Carve the duck and serve with potatoes roasted in duck fat, and perhaps a watercress and orange salad.

TAGINE DE KEFTA AU CITRON
Lamb meatballs in lemon sauce

Meatballs—but not as you know them. This Tunisian version is quite different from those you might associate with spaghetti. The ground meat is mixed with a blend of spices, and then poached in a lemony, herb-laden juice, again rich with spices.

There is one word of warning: for this dish to be truly successful, the lamb needs a little fat left in it, whereas supermarkets tend to sell it as lean as possible. You'd be better off asking a butcher to grind the meat for you. There's no frying involved and, served with rice or couscous and a salad, you still have the makings of a very healthy dish.

First make the kefta (meatballs). Into the ground lamb, mix the salt, half the black pepper, all the cayenne and cinnamon, half the cumin, three-quarters of the paprika, 2 tablespoons finely chopped parsley, and 1 heaping tablespoon grated onion.

Either pound the meat mixture in a large mortar and pestle or (much easier) give it a quick whizz in the processor—the aim is for the mixture to be very smooth. Using dampened hands, form the mixture into about 30 balls about the size of large walnuts.

Choose a large, heavy-based saucepan with a lid. Place the remaining grated onion, black pepper, cumin, and paprika in the pot with the ginger, saffron, sugar, and dried chiles. Add the water and the butter. Reserving a handful of leaves each of parsley and cilantro, tie the rest together in a bunch and add to the pot.

Bring the contents of the pot to a boil, lower the heat to a gentle simmer, cover, and cook for 20 minutes.

Now add the kefta to the sauce in the pot, together with the lemon slices and half the lemon juice. Cook uncovered for 30 minutes, turning the kefta frequently.

Check the seasoning of the sauce and finish with the remaining lemon juice, to taste. Remove the tied bunch of herbs. Chop the reserved herbs, sprinkle over the meatballs, and serve.

Serves 4

1 lb **ground lamb**

½ teaspoon **sea salt**

1 teaspoon freshly ground **black pepper**

¼ teaspoon **cayenne pepper**

½ teaspoon **ground cinnamon**

2 teaspoons **ground cumin**

1 tablespoon **sweet paprika** (this must be fresh—old paprika will make the dish taste bitter)

2 large **Spanish onions**, grated

1 teaspoon **ground ginger**

Good pinch of **saffron strands**

Good pinch of **sugar**

2–3 small **dried red chiles**

1½ cups **water**

3 tablespoons **butter**

1 small bunch **fresh, flat-leaf parsley**

1 small bunch **fresh cilantro**

1 **lemon**, sliced

½ cup **freshly squeezed lemon juice**

BISTECCA FIORENTINA WITH CHARBROILED LEMONS
Florentine steaks with lemon

Serves 4

4 **lemons**

4 large **T-bone steaks**

Sea salt and freshly ground **black pepper**

Lemons are creatures of the sun and they need to be warmed to give of their best. To juice them, first pour boiling water over them; and when you are barbecuing meat, don't forget to put some lemons on the grill. I discovered this trick recently in the Napa Valley, when the steak served for lunch at the Staglin Family Vineyard arrived with chargrilled lemons. The warmth of the lemons made that vital squeeze over the meat even sweeter.

This is a recipe for the barbecue—the lemons and meat both benefit from being grilled over charcoal, or, better still, sarments, the twigs from the vine pruning. You can, however, if desperate or in desperate weather, use a ridged griddle or skillet over a high heat.

Cut the lemons in half and season generously with salt. Place them cut side down on the hot barbecue or griddle. Cook for 10 minutes, until the lemons are scored and tender. Add the steaks and cook to taste, but they are at their best served rare. Season the cooked steaks generously and let stand for 5 minutes before serving with the lemons.

LOMO DE CERDO AL JEREZ
Pork chops with orange and sherry sauce

Serves 2

(Any more will overcrowd the skillet)

2 large, thick-cut **loin pork chops**,
    on the bone, about 11 oz each

2 **oranges**

1 cup **fino sherry**

Good pinch of **sugar**

Sea salt and freshly ground **black
    pepper**

The Spaniards love a good pig. In the Basque country, people rear the animals on a diet of acorns and cure the ham. Around Madrid they delight in eating whole suckling pig. All over the country you will find tapas of jamón serrano *(cured ham) and olives, preferably eaten mid-morning with a glass of red wine, or sherry if you are in the south. And the home of sherry, Jerez, is where this particular recipe comes from. I first tried it after a day of carousing at the Jerez horse fair, when the beautiful young men of the town ride their elegant horses up and down, occasionally inviting young women, in their flouncy flamenco dresses, to hop on the back. After such heady stuff, this was just what was called for.*

Heat a heavy-based, ridged skillet (or other heavy-based skillet) over a medium-high heat. Season the chops generously. When the skillet is very hot, add the meat. Cook for 7–8 minutes on each side, until cooked through (cut into the meat to check), but still juicy and tender.

Meanwhile, finely grate the zest of 1 orange and squeeze the juice of both. Preheat the oven to 300°F and place a serving dish inside to warm. When the chops are cooked through, transfer them to the warmed serving dish in the oven. Pour the sherry and orange juice into the skillet in which the meat cooked and turn the heat to high. Add the orange zest and sugar, and allow to bubble fiercely until reduced by half. Return the chops to the skillet, turn once to coat with the sauce, and serve immediately.

DJEJ M'QUALLI
Tagine of chicken with preserved lemon and olives

I love tagines, the slow-cooked dishes around which much Moroccan cuisine is built. Unlike many northern European stews, all the ingredients are simply put in together and simmered until the meat absorbs the flavors, making these tagines easy on the cook. And then there are the spices, and the mix of meat and dried fruits—lamb with apricots, beef with prunes. Of all the tagines, I love this classic from Marrakesh best.

Remove any excess fat from inside the chicken and wash the cavity well. Rub the crushed garlic, salt, and lemon juice into the cavity. Chop 1 tablespoon cilantro and rub into the cavity. Mix the onion, pepper, ground ginger, saffron, and olive oil, and rub over the outside of the chicken. Set aside for about 1 hour.

Place the chicken, breast-side down, in a tagine or heavy-based oval casserole dish into which it will just fit, making sure you add all the marinade juices. Pour in sufficient water to come barely halfway up the chicken and add the stick of cinnamon. Tie the remaining cilantro with a piece of string and add to the pot, with the string trailing over the side.

Bring the water to a boil, lower the heat so that it is just simmering, and cook for 1¼ hours, turning the chicken several times and, if necessary, adding a little more water to prevent it from drying out (cook with or without a lid, depending on the type of dish used). The chicken is cooked if the juices run clear when you insert a sharp knife into the angle between the leg and breast.

Rinse the olives and preserved lemons under cold running water. Cut the lemons into strips. Remove the chicken from its dish, place in an earthenware serving dish, and cover with foil to keep warm. Raise the heat to medium and let the sauce bubble for 2 minutes to reduce. Remove the cilantro and cinnamon and add the preserved lemon and olives. Simmer for 3–4 minutes to heat through, then check the seasoning—you might like to add a squeeze of lemon juice. Pour the sauce over the bird, making sure some lemon strips are draped over the breast. Let stand for 10 minutes before serving (important in Morocco, where a tagine is traditionally eaten with the fingers).

Serves 4

1 **corn-fed chicken**, about 3–3¼ lb
3 **garlic cloves**, crushed
1 teaspoon **sea salt**
¼ cup **freshly squeezed lemon juice**
1 bunch **cilantro**
1 large **white onion**, grated
1 teaspoon freshly ground **black pepper**
1 teaspoon **ground ginger**
½ teaspoon **saffron strands**
¼ cup **olive oil**
1 **stick cinnamon**
1 cup **cracked green olives**
2 **preserved lemons** (see page 120)

LADY DIANA'S SCOTCH COLLOPS
Fillet of lamb in orange sauce

Serves 4

1 lb boneless **neck of lamb**

¼ cup **butter**

1¼ cups **lamb stock**

2 **oranges**: 1 for its juice, the other
   thinly sliced

½ **onion**

Sea salt and freshly ground **black
   pepper**

Lady Diana Porter was the wife of Englishman George Porter, who earned the splendid epithet from his brother-in-law of "the best company but the worst officer that ever served the king." He was obviously a man who enjoyed life around the dining table and, happily for him, his wife seems to have been a splendid cook, if this seventeenth-century recipe is anything to go by.

Cut the lamb into slices about 1 in. across—you should have 16 pieces. Place the slices between 2 pieces of plastic wrap and beat with a rolling pin until thin and flat.

Heat half the butter in a skillet and fry the lamb slices in several batches for 1 minute on each side. Remove and set aside.

In the same skillet, heat the stock with the orange juice and the half onion. Simmer, uncovered, for 10–15 minutes, until the sauce has become slightly syrupy. Remove and discard the onion, and then beat the remaining butter into the sauce. Season the sauce well and return the fried meat to the skillet. Simmer for 5 minutes in the sauce, then add the orange slices. Simmer for a further 5 minutes before serving.

The "orange" architecture of Spain The wealth accumulated by the orange barons of Valencia in the 1920s and 1930s was such that they developed an entirely new style of architecture as they found ways to spend the proceeds from their trade. Visitors to Valencia railroad station should note the bunches of oranges that adorn the main pillars; and there are similar decorations on the art nouveau market building. But the very best examples are to be seen at the vast warehouses in Burriana, historic center of the orange trade (see also page 23).

BOEUF EN DAUBE
Braised beef

Not much orange is needed for a daube of beef, but those slivers of orange zest lend a haunting and unmistakable fragrance to this classic French beef stew. In the heat of summer daube is made with a sharp mixture of white wine, anchovies, capers, and gherkins; the winter version given here is altogether heartier, with red wine, bacon, and the brush herbs of the hillside. Cook it as slowly as possible, preferably a day in advance, and serve it on a heap of buttered noodles. Any leftover daube makes a brilliant pasta sauce.

The day before you want to cook the daube, trim any fat from the beef and discard. Going against the grain, cut the meat into 6 slices. Put the meat in a glass or earthenware bowl and add the onions, garlic, black pepper, allspice, bouquet garni, orange zest, wine, and oil. Marinate overnight (if you can leave it for 24 hours, so much the better).

The next day cut the salt pork or pancetta into lardons (cubes). Put in a large saucepan with the pork rinds or bacon, and cover with water. Bring slowly to a boil, boil for 5 minutes, and drain.

Line the base of a large, lidded earthenware or cast-iron pot with half the cooked pork rind or cooked bacon. Drain the beef, reserving the marinade. Place the beef, onions, garlic, bouquet garni, zest, and cooked salt pork in the pot, interspersed with the carrots and tomatoes. Add a little salt, carefully because of the salty pork or bacon.

Bring the reserved marinade to a boil and pour over the meat. Lay the remaining pork rind or bacon over the meat. Cover the pot with waxed paper or foil and then the lid.

Cook the daube for about 3½–4 hours, either gently simmering on the stove (which is best) or in an oven preheated to 265°F.

Toward the end of the cooking time, soak the dried mushrooms in a little warm water for about 15 minutes. Blanch the olives in boiling water for 2 minutes and drain. Add the ceps and the olives to the casserole, replace the lid, and cook for a further 30 minutes.

Before serving, skim off any surface fat and check the seasoning. The daube tastes even better if left for a day and reheated.

Serves 6

3¼ lb **chuck** or **shin of beef**, preferably in 1 piece

2 large **white onions**, quartered

3 **garlic cloves,** crushed

Good pinch of **allspice**

Bouquet garni of fresh thyme, rosemary, and bay leaf tied together

Zest of ½ **orange**, cut into strips

1 bottle robust **red wine**

2 tablespoons **olive oil**

7 oz **salt pork** or 1 thick slice **pancetta**

2 large pieces **pork rind** or 6 slices **smoked bacon**

2 large **carrots**, thickly sliced

1 lb **tomatoes**, skinned and quartered (use hot water—see page 24)

1½ cups **dried cep mushrooms**

¾ cup small **black olives** (Niçoise are good)

Sea salt and freshly ground **black pepper**

GRAINS

Pasta, pastry, breads, couscous . . . oranges and lemons find their way into a huge variety of grain-based dishes.

When it comes to American-style baking, oranges and lemons are usually associated with the sweeter end of the scale, such as cake. But elsewhere the fruits are used in all kinds of savory breads and pastries. In the eastern Mediterranean, people serve little meat pies encased in an orange pastry similar to that used for Greek spinach pie. And orange is used to scent the bread, still prepared every day in many homes. From Turkey to Pakistan, people flavor buttery, spicy pilavs with orange peel. In North Africa lemon is a favorite flavor for couscous. In Italy there is pasta sauced with lemon—a delicate, refreshing combination on a hot day—and in Provence orange is added to a fresh tomato sauce destined for a more robust pasta dish.

So, by all means use oranges and lemons in cakes, but don't forget that they marry well with all grains at every stage of the meal.

Christmas Sweet Bread (see page 69)

PENNE WITH TOMATO, ORANGE, & BASIL SAUCE

Serves 4

2¼ lb very ripe **tomatoes**

¼ cup **olive oil**

2 **garlic cloves**, finely chopped

Juice of 2 large **oranges**

1 teaspoon **tomato paste**

Pinch of **sugar**

1 **fresh bay leaf**

1 small **dried red chile**

1 bunch **fresh basil**, its leaves
     roughly torn into pieces

14 oz **dried penne**

Sea salt and freshly ground **black
     pepper**

Pecorino sardo cheese, freshly grated,
     to serve

We naturally associate pasta with Italy, but people eat almost as much of it in the South of France, particularly in the region of Nice, which, after all is just over the border and along the coast from Italy. It was in the hills behind Nice that I first learned the trick of adding orange juice to a tomato sauce to bring out its full sweetness—and a very successful trick it is too, especially if your tomatoes have not benefited from the warmth of a Provençal summer.

Here the sauce is flavored with basil and teamed with penne, but it is equally successful with fish (add a little thyme and oregano during the cooking). And I sometimes scatter in a few small black olives before serving.

Pour boiling water over the tomatoes and let stand about 30 seconds. Peel the tomatoes, cut in half, and remove all the seeds. Dice the tomato flesh roughly.

Heat the oil in a large saucepan and add the garlic. When it begins to sizzle, add the diced tomato, orange juice, tomato paste, sugar, bay leaf, chile, and seasoning. Cook for 15 minutes, stirring regularly, until the tomato has broken down. Remove from the heat and stir in the basil.

Meanwhile, bring a large saucepan of heavily salted water to a boil. Add the pasta and cook until al dente. Drain the pasta and stir into the sauce. Serve with a scattering of grated pecorino.

ORANGE PILAV

Serves 4

2¼ cups **Basmati rice** (it's important to use this type of rice)

Finely pared zest and juice of 1 large **orange**

2 large **white onions**

¼ cup **unsalted butter**

1 tablespoon **sunflower oil**

Generous pinch of **saffron strands**

3 **cardamom pods**

1 **stick of cinnamon**

3 **cloves**

10 whole **black peppercorns**

Pinch of **sugar**

1 tablespoon **orange-flower water**

1 cup **flaked almonds**

Sea salt

Pilavs, richly spiced rice cooked with butter, reached their height of popularity in the courts of the Ottoman sultans, but they are also much beloved by modern Iranians, Afghanis, and Pakistanis. This dish is based on a pilav I was served in the home of an Afghani carpet trader in Lahore. I was allowed to enter the kitchen, where the women of the house soon tore off their veils and started giggling. Meanwhile, the men sat next door having a serious business discussion.

The care with which that pilav was prepared showed the honor being done to us as guests. The orange zest, combined with the expensive spices and the orange-flower water, lends a delicate, haunting fragrance to the rice. This is an excellent dish to accompany broiled meats or roast chicken.

Soak the rice in plenty of water for at least 1 hour. Drain and rinse well several times to remove any remaining starch.

Bring a saucepan of water to a boil and blanch the orange zest for 2 minutes. Drain, reserving the zest.

Cut the onions into fine half moons. In a heavy-based, wide saucepan large enough to cook all the pilav in, melt half the butter with the oil over a gentle heat. Add the onions and fry gently, stirring often, until the onions are tender and golden—this takes about 10 minutes.

Bring a kettle of water to a boil. Steep the saffron in 2 tablespoons of the water for about 10 minutes. Reserve the rest of the water.

Add the rice to the saucepan with the onions and stir well to coat all the grains with fat. Add the saffron, cardamom, cinnamon, cloves, peppercorns, sugar, and a generous measure of salt, and stir again. Mix in the orange zest and juice and the orange-flower water. Add 2¼ cups boiled water (or slightly more, depending on the freshness of the rice and how soft you like it). Bring the pilav to a boil, then lower the heat to a simmer. Cook for 10–12 minutes, until all the liquid has been absorbed and small holes appear in the surface of the rice. Then turn off the heat, cover the pot with a clean dish towel, and let stand for 5 minutes.

Meanwhile, melt the remaining butter and carefully fry the almonds until just golden. Remove the dish towel, pour the melted butter and almonds over the pilav, fluff up the rice with a fork, and serve.

CHRISTMAS SWEET BREAD

I love the sweet Christmas breads made in Italy and the South of France. Studded with nuts and dried fruit, thick with orange and lemon peel, with a whiff of alcohol and a dusting of spice, this is what I want to eat by the fireside on Christmas Eve. You don't have to make this months in advance and it keeps well in an airtight container. Don't be alarmed by the shape: it should be flattish. (Photograph on page 64)

Sift the flour and salt carefully and put in a warm place in a large bowl. Prepare the yeast according to the instructions on the package.

Warm the milk until tepid (test with your finger). Make a well in the center of the flour and pour in the milk and yeast. Mix to a dough—you may need to add a little warm water. Work it well with floured hands for 5 minutes, then sprinkle the surface with flour, cover with a clean dish towel, and set in a warm place for about 1 hour to rise.

Roughly chop the apricots and add to the sultanas, then pour the Cognac or grappa over them and set aside.

Preheat the oven to 225°F. Bring a saucepan of water to a boil and plunge in the zest; drain as soon as the water returns to a boil. Sprinkle the zest over a baking sheet and place in the oven for 15 minutes to dry. Add the dried zest, chopped almonds, sugar, and egg yolks to the apricots and sultanas.

Chop the butter into small pieces and work into the dough a little at a time. When all the butter is incorporated, stir in the fruit mixture, using a wooden spoon. Work gently so as not to knock the air out of the dough. If necessary, sprinkle with a little more flour. Place the dough in a rough round shape on a large metal baking sheet. Cover with a cloth, place in a warm spot, and let rise again until at least doubled in size.

Preheat the oven to 350°F and bake the risen dough for 30 minutes. Lower the temperature to 325°F and bake for another 30 minutes. Test with a skewer: if it comes out clean, the bread is done; if not, bake for another 10 minutes. There should be a good ratio of crust to bread. Let the bread cool, then dust with confectioner's sugar and cinnamon. Serve in long, thin slices—perhaps with a glass of vin santo or lemon liqueur (see page 138).

Serves plenty

6½ cups **all-purpose flour**

Good pinch of **sea salt**

1 envelope **active dry yeast**

1½ cups **whole milk**

⅔ cup **dried, pre-soaked apricots**

⅔ cup **sultanas** or **golden raisins**

3 tablespoons **Cognac** (you can also use **Grappa**)

Zest of 1 large **sweet orange**, coarsely chopped

Zest of 1 **lemon**, coarsely chopped

1 cup **skinned, chopped almonds**

½ cup **superfine sugar**

3 large **egg yolks**

1 cup **unsalted butter**

Confectioner's sugar

Ground cinnamon

LEMON COUSCOUS

Correctly made, couscous Moroccan style is a work of art. The grain is first picked over by hand and then steamed, massaged again by hand (how the women cooks don't burn their fingers as they rake over the scorching grain I do not know), steamed for a second time, and then piled high to form a base for the braised vegetables that accompany it. Exquisite, but hard work.

This dish is an altogether simpler affair, perfect for hot summer evenings, perhaps to accompany some barbecued meats or, better still, the spicy lamb sausage known as merguez. It relies on the precooked grain (the kind mostly widely available here) that needs nothing more than soaking in hot water, flavoring with spices, and dressing in olive oil. There are chickpeas for bulk and texture, raisins for sweetness, and lemon zest and juice to give the dish a lift. The final touch of caramelized onions is essential.

Serves 4

1 large **Spanish onion**
¼ cup **olive oil**
1¼ cups **instant couscous**
½ cup **currants**
1 teaspoon **salt**
½ teaspoon **ground ginger**
½ teaspoon **ground cinnamon**
14-oz **can chickpeas**, drained
2 **lemons**: zest and juice from 1 lemon; the other lemon cut into fine slices
½ teaspoon **saffron strands**

Chop the onion into fine half moons. Cook the onion in half the olive oil over a medium heat for 30 minutes, stirring occasionally, until the onions are lightly caramelized.

Meanwhile, stir the currants, salt, ginger, and cinnamon, remaining olive oil, drained chickpeas, and lemon zest and juice into the couscous. Boil about 1 cup water and steep the saffron in it for a few minutes.

Pour the hot saffron water over the couscous mixture, cover with a dish towel, and steam for 5–10 minutes. Fluff up with a fork. Scatter the caramelized onions and lemon slices on top and let stand for at least 1 hour before serving.

TAGLIOLINI AL LIMONE
Pasta with lemon sauce

Serves 2

2 **lemons**

½ cup fruity **Italian white wine**

9 oz **fresh egg tagliolini** (you can also use tagliatelle)

1 cup **heavy cream**

1 cup freshly grated **Parmesan cheese**

White pepper

Salt

I first tasted this on Italy's Amalfi coast, in a restaurant looking out to sea, its back to the steep hillside terraces where Amalfi lemons are grown. It was the end of winter and the scent of the lemons hung heavy in the air. This simple dish could not have been bettered—and it wasn't just the setting.
(Photograph on opening pages of book)

Finely grate the zest of the lemons, making sure you don't include any of the bitter white pith. Add all but 1 teaspoon of the zest to the white wine in a small saucepan. Bring to a boil and simmer until the wine is reduced by half. Let cool slightly.

Bring a large saucepan of salted water to a boil for the pasta. Meanwhile, beat the cream into the wine and lemon zest, adding white pepper and a little salt to taste. Place the pasta in the boiling water and return the sauce to a low heat, stirring regularly.

When the sauce is warmed through, remove from the heat and stir in three-quarters of the Parmesan. As soon as the pasta is al dente (2–3 minutes if truly fresh, as opposed to supermarket-chilled), drain and combine with the sauce. Spoon onto warmed plates, sprinkle with the remaining lemon zest and Parmesan, and serve.

Growing lemons around Amalfi

The steep coastline that rises above the resort of Amalfi, in southern Italy, is not just one of Europe's most scenic stretches, it is also home to some of the very best lemons in the world. These lemons are grown on terraces that cling perilously to the hillside, carved out specially to grow the fruit; and they are covered by thick black netting to shield them from harmful frosts. Amalfi lemons are harvested during the early months of the year and on a crisp January day their sweet fragrance fills the sharp air.

POMPE A L'HUILE
Provençal olive oil bread

The French and Italians are rightly famed for a wide range of delicious breads, both sweet and savory. This lovely olive oil bread is perfumed with orange and lemon zest, and is traditionally cooked in a round, with a hole at its center.

Mix together the flour, yeast, salt, and sugar. Add the orange and lemon zest. Make a well in the center of the flour and add the oil and whole eggs. Combine with a wooden spoon and then slowly add 1¼ cups of warm water until you have a sticky mixture—make sure you don't overdo the water.

With well-floured hands, and on a floured surface, knead the dough well for 6–7 minutes, until it is smooth and pliant. Cover with a heavy cloth and set in a warm place to rise for about 5 hours or overnight.

When you return to the dough, it should have doubled or even tripled in size. Now punch it down, knocking out all the air and returning the dough to its original size. Spread it on a lightly oiled baking sheet in a circle and make a hole in the middle. Place a greased heatproof cup or small round mold in this hole. Cover the dough and let rise again for 1–2 hours.

Preheat the oven to 375°F. Mix the egg yolk with 2 tablespoons cold water and brush all over the surface of the bread. Bake in the center of the oven for 30–40 minutes, until nicely golden; pierce with a skewer to make sure it is thoroughly baked—the skewer should come out clean. Remove the mold and cool the bread on a rack before serving.

Serves plenty
6 cups **bread flour**
1 envelope **active dry yeast**
2 teaspoons **sea salt**
1 teaspoon **white sugar**
Zest of 1 **orange**
Zest of 1 **lemon**
¼ cup **olive oil**
3 **whole eggs** plus 1 **egg yolk**

SPANAKOPITTA
Spinach pie

Serves 6–8

2¼ cups **all-purpose flour**

2 small **oranges**

6 tablespoons **olive oil**

1 large **egg**

1¾ lb **fresh spinach**

1 **onion**, finely chopped

1 teaspoon **ground cumin**

¼ cup **frshly squeezed lemon juice**

3 tablespoons chopped **fresh dill**

2 tablespoons **sesame seeds**

Sea salt and **freshly ground black pepper**

The Greeks love picnics and this pie is a favorite for such occasions. Spinach and orange is a well-loved combination as a vegetable dish (see recipe on page 87), but what makes the difference in this recipe is the use of orange juice in the sesame-seed encrusted pastry; the spinach itself is combined with lemon juice. As befits a picnic, this pie should be served as though lightly warmed by the sun—neither too cold nor too hot.

Sift the flour with 1 teaspoon salt. Grate the zest from 1 orange and squeeze and strain the juice from both. Make a well in the center of the flour and add 2 tablespoons olive oil and the orange juice and zest. Separate the egg; reserve the yolk and lightly whisk the white.

Add the egg white to the flour and work them together. With floured hands, knead the dough for 10 minutes, until smooth and pliable rather than sticky. Wrap in plastic wrap and chill for about 1 hour.

Remove the stalks from the spinach and wash the leaves very well. Drain, then put the spinach in a pot, cover, and cook over a low heat for 12–15 minutes until thoroughly wilted. Drain the spinach again and, when it is cool enough to handle, squeeze it dry very thoroughly.

Heat 2 tablespoons oil in the saucepan over a gentle heat and add the onion. Cook for 10 minutes until the onion is soft. Add the spinach, plenty of seasoning, the cumin, lemon juice, and dill. Cook gently for a further 5 minutes, until any remaining liquid has evaporated.

Preheat the oven to 350°F and prepare a little ice water. Roll out two-thirds of the pastry to fit an oiled tart pan about 8–9 in. diameter. Trim the edges and fill the pie with the spinach mixture. Roll out the remaining pastry and place it over the surface of the pie, joining the edges with some ice water. Brush the surface of the pie with the remaining oil and bake for 30 minutes.

Remove the pie from the oven and lower the heat to 300°F. Brush the surface of the pastry with the beaten egg yolk and sprinkle with sesame seeds. Bake for a further 30 minutes, until the sesame seeds are lightly toasted. Let cool before serving in thick slices, just warm.

MOROCCAN BREAKFAST BREAD

Makes 12 rolls

1 **orange**

6 cups **bread flour**

½ cup **sugar**

Good pinch of **sea salt**

2 tablespoons **sesame seeds**

2 tablespoons **poppy seeds**

1 tablespoon **fennel seeds**

1 envelope **active dry yeast**

½ cup **unsalted butte**r, roughly chopped

3 tablespoons **orange-flower water**

1 **egg yolk**

If you want to know where the bakery is in a Moroccan city, follow the small boys who wend their way through the narrow streets with trays of dough, neatly covered with cloths, perched on their heads—in the medieval alleyways of Marrakesh and Fez the communal baker still plies his trade.

Each Moroccan baker has his own recipe, but orange-flower water and different seeds make a regular appearance, especially for the sweeter breads favored for breakfast, to be served with honey or perhaps some fig conserve. I must be honest: I do not often bake my own bread, but these light, slightly spicy rolls are well worth the effort. Of course, the Moroccan baker would probably be horrified by the use of yeast from an envelope.

Finely peel the zest of the orange, preferably with a zester. Put the zest in a large mixing bowl with the flour, sugar, salt, all the seeds, and yeast. Heat 2 cups water in a saucepan. When it is hot, add the butter and orange-flower water. Stir until the butter has melted. Set aside this buttery liquid for about 20 minutes to cool to room temperature.

Make a well in the center of the flour and add about a quarter of the buttery liquid. Stir in well with a wooden spoon. Continue slowly stirring in the rest of the liquid until it is all absorbed and you have a sticky dough. Dust your hands with flour and briefly knead the dough for 1–2 minutes. Cover with a clean dish towel and let rise for 2 hours—it should double in size.

Punch down the dough with your fist to expel air and then set aside to rise again. After 2 hours give it a quick knead and then divide it roughly into 12 balls. Shape each ball into a flattened round and place on a lightly buttered baking sheet, leaving a gap between each roll so that they do not stick together as they rise. Cover with the dish towel and set aside to rise again.

When you are ready to bake the rolls, preheat the oven to 400°F. Beat the egg yolk with 2 tablespoons water and brush this mixture over the surface of the rolls. Prick each roll once or twice with a skewer or carving fork. Place in the oven and bake for 20 minutes, until golden and with a slight crust. Shake to make sure they do not stick to the baking sheet, then let cool.

FETTUCINE WITH ROQUEFORT, LEMON, & ROSEMARY

This recipe is based on one that food writer Patricia Wells picked up in Germany, but it seems more at home in Provence, where she has her much-loved farmhouse home. It is brilliant quick food, perfect for an indulgent supper when you don't really feel like cooking. The combination of the salty cheese, aromatic rosemary, and sharp lemon juice against the slippery pasta is truly inspired.

Put a large saucepan of water (at least 6 quarts) and 1 tablespoon sea salt on to boil.

Mash the butter and the Roquefort cheese together with a fork until you have a smooth paste.

Grate the lemon zest and then slice the flesh thinly. Strip the needles from the sprigs of rosemary and chop them finely—you should have about 2 heaping teaspoons. Mix the lemon zest with the chopped rosemary, then add a generous grating of nutmeg and a good grind of black pepper.

When the water is boiling vigorously, add the pasta. The exact cooking time will depend on the type—truly fresh egg pasta will take only 2–3 minutes (taste to check), but the kind that is sold refrigerated in supermarkets usually takes at least 4–5 minutes.

When the pasta is to your taste (or "to your tooth," as the Italians say), place the 4 bowls in which you will serve it in the sink and drain the pasta directly over them, catching a reasonable amount of water—you will need around 2 full ladles. This both warms the bowls and, even more vitally, allows you to keep some of the cooking water. Put aside 2 ladles of cooking water and discard the rest. Put the pasta back into the pot. Carefully stir in the butter-and-Roquefort mixture and add 1 ladle cooking water. Stir together well, adding a little more water as necessary to achieve the desired consistency of sauce. Sprinkle in the lemon-and-rosemary mixture and toss thoroughly.

Serve in the warmed bowls, with a slice of lemon placed on top of each helping of pasta.

Serves 4

3 tablespoons **unsalted butter**

3 oz **Roquefort cheese**

1 **lemon**

2 small sprigs **fresh rosemary**

1 **nutmeg**, for grating

12 oz fresh **egg fettucine** or **tagliatelle**

Sea salt and freshly ground **black pepper**

Note: This is a quick dish to prepare, but it is made much easier if you start with the butter and cheese at room temperature.

TABBOULEH

You can't have a meal in the Lebanon without a bowl of tabbouleh, the dish of bulgur wheat mixed with herbs, lemon juice, and olive oil that many people would describe as the national dish (though really that honor should go to kibbeh). Even if you avoid the mezze stage and choose just some broiled fish or a kebab or two, you're likely to get a little bowl of this salad—whether or not you've ordered it. But don't get cross, for the waiter knows what he is doing. The dressing should be distinctly sharp, producing a dish that is perfect for cleansing and refreshing the palate after the heavy, perhaps slightly greasy, meat or fish.

If you serve tabbouleh as part of a mixed mezze, do as the Lebanese do and accompany it with crisp leaves of romaine lettuce rather than bread to scoop it up.

Serves 4

¾ cup **bulgur wheat**

½ cup **freshly squeezed lemon juice**

¼ cup **extra-virgin olive oil**

1 large bunch **fresh, flat-leaf parsley**

1 bunch **fresh mint**

1 small bunch **fresh dill**

6 **scallions**

Sea salt and freshly ground **black pepper**

Barely cover the bulgur wheat with warm, boiled water and soak for about 10 minutes, until it has absorbed the water and swollen.

Beat together the lemon juice and olive oil, and season generously before pouring over the bulgur wheat.

Discard the stalks of the parsley, mint, and dill, and very finely chop the leaves. Very finely chop the scallions and add to the wheat with the herbs. Let stand for at least 30 minutes, to allow all the flavors to mingle, before serving.

VEGETABLES & SALADS

Many vegetables need the touch of citric acid. The easiest example is the salad dressing—and not just for lettuce leaves, but for cooked vegetables to be served warm as salads. By all means use vinegar, but I prefer lemon juice. And sometimes quite a lot of it, as in Lebanese fattoush.

There are also occasions when the fruits themselves can be the main ingredient of a salad. In Sicily people eat salads of orange, dressed with just olive oil, salt and pepper, scattered with black olives; in Morocco the same treatment is given to lemons. And in Seville juicy segments of orange are combined with lettuce, olives, and anchovies for the perfect lunch for one. Back in North Africa, carrot and orange salad is a sweetly perfumed affair.

Then there are those cooked dishes where the fruit is integral to the cooking process. Chief among these are the classic artichoke dishes of the Mediterranean—you need the lemon juice to prevent the artichoke from discoloring. In Sicily the cooks add orange juice as well. Try a squeeze of orange over spinach dressed with olive oil or cooked in plenty of butter and cream.

Moroccan Lemon & Olive Salad (see page 90)

ENSALADA SEVILLANA
Seville salad

Serves 4

2 **baby romaine lettuces**

2 large **oranges**

1 small **red onion**

2 tablespoons **capers**, drained
and rinsed

⅓ cup **cracked green olives**

8 **anchovy fillets**

1 **garlic clove**

Good pinch of **sea salt**

1 **hard-boiled egg yolk**

2 tablespoons **sherry vinegar**

½ cup **extra-virgin olive oil**

1 tablespoon finely chopped
fresh tarragon

Freshly ground **black pepper**

Tarragon sprigs, to garnish (optional)

This is one of those salads that is a meal in itself, perfect for lunch on a hot day, washed down with a well-chilled glass of fino sherry. Not that any self-respecting Spaniard would regard this as sufficient—it would merely be the precursor to a sizeable hunk of meat or fish. Followed by a siesta, of course.

Cut each lettuce in half lengthwise. Peel the oranges and slice them across into fine rings and then half moons. Chop the onion very finely.

Place each lettuce half on an individual serving plate and scatter the orange pieces, the capers, and the olives on top. Drape 2 anchovy fillets over each half of lettuce.

To make the dressing, crush the garlic clove with the salt, then mash it with the egg yolk until you have a smooth paste. Beat in the sherry vinegar and add black pepper to taste. Drip in the olive oil slowly, beating all the time to amalgamate thoroughly. Finish the dressing with the fresh tarragon, pour over the salad, and serve, garnished with tarragon sprigs if you like.

ARTICHOKE HEARTS WITH ORANGES & LEMONS

Serves 4

4 large **globe artichokes**

¾ cup **freshly squeezed lemon juice**

½ **lemon** for rubbing over cut artichoke surfaces

2 large **Spanish onions**

Juice of 4 large **sweet oranges**

¼ cup **white wine vinegar**

½ cup **extra-virgin olive oil**

¼ cup **capers**, drained and rinsed

4 **anchovy fillets**

2 tablespoons **sugar**

Sea salt

The Sicilians grow big, fat oranges, wonderful knobbly lemons, and gloriously fresh purple globe artichokes. Some of the best capers in the world come from the island of Pantelleria, off the Sicilian coast, halfway to Tunisia; and the sea is full of sparkling silver anchovies. On the salt flats near Trapani on the eastern coast they make the best salt for preserving these fish. And they have some pretty good olive oil, too. Put it all together and you have a sensational dish. The balance of sweet and sour is typically Sicilian.

Prepare the artichoke hearts. Remove the hearts from the artichokes by first snapping off the outer leaves—they will break off at the base. Leaving a good section of stalk, cut across the artichoke just above the heart. With a sharp knife, remove the hairy choke and quickly rub the cut surface with the half lemon to prevent the artichoke from discoloring. Peel the stalk. The fresher the artichoke, the easier it is to remove the leaves and peel the stalk.

Bring a large saucepan of well-salted water and ¼ cup lemon juice to a boil, and blanch the artichoke hearts for 3 minutes. Drain thoroughly.

Chop the onions across into fine half-moons. Place half the onions across the base of a heavy-based flameproof casserole dish and arrange the artichoke hearts on top, stalk side up. Scatter over the remaining onions and add all the orange juice and the remaining lemon juice, the vinegar, the olive oil, and enough water to just cover the artichokes. Season generously with salt, bring to a boil and then simmer uncovered for 30 minutes or until the artichoke hearts are extremely tender.

Remove the artichokes, retaining the cooking liquid, and set aside in a large earthenware serving bowl. Add the capers, anchovy fillets, and sugar to the cooking liquid and simmer for 10–15 minutes, stirring regularly, until you have a thick sauce. Pour over the hearts and let cool before serving—overnight is best.

FATTOUSH

I love tabbouleh (see page 79), but I think I love the other Lebanese classic, fattoush, even more. Perhaps it is to do with the crisply toasted, casually broken pieces of flat bread that lurk beneath the lettuce, cucumber, scallions, and tomatoes. As with the classic Tuscan bread salad, panzanella, the pieces of bread absorb the oily, lemony dressing but somehow retain their crunch. There is also the scattering of sumac and pomegranate seeds, and of segments of lemon—mouth-puckering against the sweet pepperiness of the herbs. If there is a more refreshing, restorative salad, I'd like to know about it. (Fattoush is shown served with Lemon-marinated Chicken Wings in the photograph on page 55)

Quarter the cherry tomatoes. Chop the cucumber into slices about ⅜ in. thick and then into quarters. Chop the scallions into ½-in. chunks, including all of the green part. Cut the lettuce leaves into ½-in. strips, discarding the stalk. Finely chop the leaves of the fresh mint and parsley. If you have purslane, strip the leaves from the fleshy stalks.

Slice the unleavened bread and toast it—briefly in a hot oven or broiler—until crisp. Place the toasted bread in the bottom of the bowl in which you will be serving your salad.

Beat together the lemon juice and salt, and then slowly amalgamate the oil, whisking all the time. Mix together all the vegetables and herbs, place over the bread pieces in the bowl, and then add the lemon-and-oil dressing. Scatter the sumac and pomegranate seeds and the segments of lemon flesh over the top and serve.

Serves 4

7 oz **cherry tomatoes**

1 miniature **cucumber**

8 small or 4 large **scallions**

8 large leaves **romaine lettuce**

Small bunch **fresh mint,** preferably spearmint

Large bunch **fresh, flat-leaf parsley**

Small bunch **purslane**, if available

1 large round **unleavened Arabic bread (khobz)**

¼ cup **freshly squeezed emon juice**

¼ teaspoon **sea salt**

¼ cup **extra-virgin olive oil**

2 tablespoons **sumac seeds** or **pomegranate seeds** (or both if available)

½ **lemon**, peeled and the flesh cut into small segments

CREAMED SPINACH WITH ORANGE

In her book Good Things, *a collection of recipes made with her favorite ingredients, the admirable Jane Grigson picks out a recipe like this one from an eighteenth-century cookbook. Although she describes the combination of spinach and orange as "unusual," it was common at that time to finish the cooking of many vegetables with a squeeze of orange juice. Spinach and orange are an especially happy marriage, whether in soup or as a vegetable dish. By the way, she also stresses the need to wash the spinach very thoroughly, advice that must be emphasized—there's nothing worse than a mouthful of gritty leaves.*

This is a rich dish and for maximum enjoyment it should really be served in the French manner—that is, on its own as either an appetizer or as a vegetable dish to follow some plain broiled meat or fish.

Serves 4

1 lb **fresh spinach**

1 **nutmeg**, for grating

1½ cups **heavy cream**

Juice of 1 **Seville orange**

1 large **sweet orange**

4 thin slices **white bread**, crusts removed

3 tablespoons **butter**

Sea salt and freshly ground **black pepper**

Wash the spinach very well and drain thoroughly. Place it in a large, heavy-based pot with a lid over a low heat. Do not add any water; the spinach needs only the remaining drops of rinsing water in which to cook. Cook for 15 minutes, stirring regularly, until the spinach has completely wilted. Refresh in cold water and drain well, squeezing the spinach against the colander with the back of a wooden spoon to get rid of as much liquid as possible.

Wipe the pot clean and return the spinach to it. Season well with salt and pepper and add a pinch of grated nutmeg. Stir in the cream.

Place over a low heat and cook, uncovered, for 35–40 minutes, stirring regularly, until the spinach has absorbed all the cream. Meanwhile, preheat the oven to 300°F to warm a serving dish. Remove the spinach from the heat, transfer to the warmed serving dish, and add the juice of the Seville orange.

Cut the bread into triangles and fry in the butter until crisp and golden. Cut the sweet orange into quarters. Serve the spinach with the fried bread on the side and the orange quarters to squeeze over.

ARTICHOKE, FAVA BEAN, & LEMON SALAD

Serves 4

2¼ lb young, early season **fava beans in their pods**

4 small **globe artichokes**, still tightly closed

⅔ cup **freshly squeezed lemon juice**

½ lemon, for rubbing over cut artichoke surfaces

Extra-virgin olive oil

1 heaping tablespoon chopped **fresh mint**

1 heaping tablespoon chopped **fresh dill**

Sea salt and freshly ground **black pepper**

lemon quarters, to serve (optional)

Globe artichokes and fava beans happily come into season together, as good Greek cooks know. They are a marriage made in heaven. Marinated in plenty of lemon juice and olive oil, this is possibly my favorite salad of all time. It certainly deserves to be served all on its own as an appetizer.

Shell the beans. Remove the hearts from the globe artichokes as described on page 84, but this time also remove the stalks. Place the hearts in a bowl of cold water into which you have added 3 tablespoons of the lemon juice.

Bring a large saucepan of salted water to a boil. Drain the artichoke hearts and boil them for 10–15 minutes, until they are tender—the exact timing will depend on their size and freshness. Drain, cut into quarters, and place in a serving bowl (preferably one made of earthenware) into which they just fit.

Bring another saucepan of salted water to a boil and add the fava beans. Cook for 2–3 minutes, until just tender, no more. Drain and scatter over the artichoke hearts.

Pour the remaining lemon juice over the salad, followed by sufficient olive oil to barely cover the artichoke hearts. Season well and keep at room temperature for at least 4 hours—preferably overnight. Sprinkle the salad with the chopped fresh mint and dill, and serve with extra quarters of lemon for squeezing over the salad, if you like.

SALADE DE CITRON ET OLIVES
Moroccan lemon and olive salad

Serves 4

3 very ripe **unwaxed lemons**,
  preferably thin-skinned

1 teaspoon **paprika**

1 teaspoon **ground cumin**

Good pinch of **cayenne pepper**

1 teaspoon **sugar**

1 **red onion**, finely chopped

¼ cup **fresh, flat-leaf parsley**

¼ cup **extra-virgin olive oil**

16 **black** or **violet olives** (Greek
  Kalamata olives are a good choice)

Sea salt

Lemons in a salad? Isn't that just too mouth-puckering? The answer is no—providing you have very ripe lemons, lots of fruity olive oil, some sweet black olives, finely chopped red onion, and a generous scattering of fresh parsley. The first time I tried this salad, eating beside the harbor in the pretty Moroccan port of Essaouira, it was a revelation. It is a perfect match for broiled sardines.

The Sicilians serve thinly sliced lemons sprinkled with wild arugula, sliced red onion, and fresh thyme, and dressed with extra-virgin olive oil. They also make a fine orange salad of peeled, sliced oranges scattered with small black olives; in Morocco a similar salad is sprinkled with cinnamon and paprika. (Photograph on page 80)

Peel the lemons and soak them in heavily salted water for 1 hour. Drain and finely dice the flesh, discarding any seeds. Mix in the paprika, cumin, and cayenne pepper, plus the sugar, chopped onion, parsley, and olive oil. Chill well before serving, sprinkled with the olives.

Words from the Moorish calendar . . .
Various references to oranges and lemons are found in Moorish literature. This piece of advice comes from an agricultural calendar: "Where there are doorways or basins and pools then plant round about such trees as laurel, myrtle, cypress, pine, citron, jasmine, Seville orange, grapefruit, lime, and cane-apple, for these never shed their leaves. And on the largest of these trees hang trellises and bowers for your pleasure, and by the same means you may shade pools of water so they remain cool."

Extract taken from "The Moorish Calendar," translated from the twelfth-century *Book of Agriculture* (*Kitab al Felaha*) by Yahya ibn al Awam

FRIED EGGPLANT WITH SWEET PEPPERS & PRESERVED LEMONS

I first ate this salad in Fez, the Moroccan town where Monty Python's Life of Brian *was shot on location and which retains a suitably absurd, medieval feel. The streets of the town are so narrow that often the heavily laden donkeys can only just fit through, their guides all the time shouting out "balek, balek," which translates roughly as "watch out." Yet behind these narrow, dark streets lie gracious mansions set around courtyards filled with tinkling fountains and shaded by orange and lemon trees.*

It was in a courtyard in Fez that I enjoyed a spectacular lunch of delicately spiced and scented salads, served with nothing more than warm bread and cool water. I begged the recipe for this eggplant version, intrigued by its smoky flavor, which I found came from the broiled peppers. Long, sweet peppers are better in this dish than the more ordinary bell peppers.

Serves 4

3 **eggplant**s

Sunflower oil, preferably unrefined

3 long, sweet **red peppers**

½ cup **freshly squeezed lemon juice**

1 teaspoon **ground cumin**

1 teaspoon **paprika**

1 **garlic clove**, finely chopped

Generous handful of chopped **fresh, flat-leaf parsley**

Sugar

¼ **preserved lemon**, rinsed and finely chopped (see page 121)

Sea salt

Slice the eggplants into rounds ¾ in. thick. Fill a non-stick skillet with sunflower oil to a depth of about ¾ in. and place over a medium heat. When the oil is very hot, add the rounds of eggplant in 4–5 batches; to prevent eggplants from absorbing too much fat, never overcrowd the skillet and always use very hot oil. Fry for 1–2 minutes on each side, until nicely browned, and drain on paper towels.

Preheat the broiler. When it is at maximum heat, broil the peppers until their skin is blackened all over. Place in a sealed plastic bag for about 10 minutes and then scrape off the blackened skin. Cut open, remove and discard the seeds and core, and roughly chop the flesh.

Cut the drained eggplants into quarters and mix with the chopped pepper in a wide earthenware serving dish. Add the lemon juice, the cumin and paprika, the garlic and the chopped parsley, and a generous sprinkling of both salt and sugar. Sprinkle with the preserved lemon and set aside for several hours before serving.

MOROCCAN CARROT & ORANGE SALAD

For me, one of the most extraordinary features of Moroccan food are the sweet salads that precede the tagines, the slow-cooked dishes named after the conical cooking pot in which they are traditionally prepared (see the chicken and lemon tagine on page 61). These salads are redolent of the exotic flavors of the souk, with their herbs, spices, and perfumes. One of the simplest is a salad of carrots and oranges, scented with orange-flower water and sprinkled with sugar and cinnamon. It's a remarkably successful combination, and extremely refreshing when served well chilled.

Tomato and orange salad is another good idea (choose tomatoes that are as full flavored as possible), especially when dressed with a honey vinaigrette. And orange juice is a fine addition to a dish of carrots—cooked whole, thickly sliced, and dressed with the juice and some olive oil while still warm.

Peel the carrots and cut out the tough, lighter colored orange core. Finely grate the remaining carrot flesh.

Peel the oranges carefully and then roughly chop their flesh, retaining all of their juice.

Mix the oranges, their juice, and the carrots together. Add the orange-flower water, sugar, cinnamon, lemon juice, olive oil, and plenty of salt, and mix again. Garnish with the black olives and chill well before serving.

Serves 4

1 lb large **carrots**

3 large **oranges**

2 tablespoons **orange-flower water**

1 tablespoon **superfine sugar**

½ teaspoon **ground cinnamon**

¼ cup **freshly squeezed lemon juice**

¼ cup **extra-virgin olive oil**

8 **black olives**, to garnish

Sea salt

DESSERTS

I have a confession to make. I have not included any cakes. The only bit of pastry appears around the essential lemon tart. There is a rice pudding, but it is Portuguese.

When I told friends I was writing a book about oranges and lemons, many of them said "Oh—desserts, then." Yet I wanted to show how essential these fruit are to the cooking of the Mediterranean at all stages of the meal. And the Mediterranean countries do not have a tradition of desserts in the same way we do. They tend to end their meals with something fruit-based (often just a bowl of fruit on ice; try serving cherries that way) and keep the pastries, cookies, and various sweetmeats to nibble at mid-morning, with coffee.

So when it comes to desserts, I prefer to err on the side of simplicity. A dish of figs baked in orange juice, an icy granita of lemon, a salad of oranges dusted with cinnamon and sprinkled with orange-flower water— these are the things I prefer to end my meal with. If you must have something truly wicked, try the lemon syllabub.

Lemon Water Ice (see page 98)

TARTE AU CITRON
French lemon tart

Serves 6–8

FOR THE PASTRY

2¼ cups **all-purpose flour**

½ cup **superfine sugar**

½ cup **unsalted butter**, at room temperature

1 **egg yolk**

¼ cup **ice water**

FOR THE FILLING

4 large **eggs**, separated

⅔ cup **superfine sugar**

3 **unwaxed lemons**

1 heaping teaspoon **cornstarch**

A tarte au citron is a thing of beauty. I am not thinking of a perfectly scalloped, blow-torched, sugar-dusted restaurant version, but a rough-hewn circle of pastry, so buttery that its edges are almost crumbling, its surface wobbly to the touch, the deep yellow flecked with brown where it has caught the oven's heat. Why not just call it lemon tart? Because I have eaten the very best ones in France. Maybe it is something to do with the lemons, but somehow I don't think so.

Sift the flour and sugar together. Cut the butter into small pieces and, using your fingers, crumble it into the flour and sugar. Stir in the egg yolk and enough of the ice water to make a dough. Work quickly with your hands until the dough is smooth (timing—and cold hands—are of the essence), then wrap in plastic wrap and chill for about 45 minutes.

Meanwhile, prepare the filling. Beat together the 4 egg yolks and three-quarters of the sugar. Zest, then juice the lemons, and add both the zest and juice to the egg mixture. Carefully stir in the cornstarch, making sure there are no lumps, and transfer the mixture to a saucepan. Heat over a medium-low heat for 10 minutes, stirring continuously, until the mixture thickens. Do not allow it to boil or the mixture will curdle. When it has thickened, remove from the heat and allow to cool.

Preheat the oven to 350°F. On a floured board, roll out the pastry sufficiently to fill a deep, buttered tart pan 8–9in. in diameter. A deep pan is important here because the filling rises. Leave extra pastry hanging over the edge, as it shrinks during cooking. Prick the base all over with a fork and place in the oven for 15 minutes.

Meanwhile, beat the egg whites with the remaining sugar for the filling until very stiff. Carefully fold the egg whites into the lemon custard and pour gently into the cooked tart shell. Return the tart to the oven and bake for about 25 minutes, until the top is lightly browned and the filling risen. Remove and let cool before serving; don't worry if it cracks slightly.

GRANITA DI LIMONE
Lemon water ice

Serves 4

1 cup **superfine sugar**

1¼ cups **water**

1½ cups **freshly squeezed lemon juice**

4 small sprigs **fresh mint**, to decorate

The Sicilians don't like to admit it, but they learned the art of making ice cream from Moorish invaders. It was the latter who first made the cooling iced drinks that were the precursor of the granita (see page 134). It was also, incidentally, the Moors who revived the irrigation canals left by the Romans and so enabled the planting of the citrus groves for which Sicily is now justly famous. To give an Arabic touch, I serve my lemon granita with a sprig of mint.

An orange granita is also delightful, especially if the syrup is delicately scented with a little orange-flower water before freezing. And the juice of blood oranges makes for a particularly fine granita. (Photograph on page 94)

Mix the sugar with the water. Bring to a boil and simmer uncovered for 5 minutes. Set the syrup aside to cool.

Mix the lemon juice with the sugar syrup and place in the freezer. Stir every 15 minutes for 2 hours, then every 30 minutes for 1 hour, or until the granita has nearly frozen solid but still has a slightly slushy consistency. If you wish to leave the granita in the freezer for longer, remove it at least 1 hour before serving so that it is not set solid.

Serve decorated with the sprigs of mint.

FLAN DE NARANJA
Orange egg custard

We associate crème caramel with France but, if anything, the Spanish are even greater lovers of the egg custard. Barcelona is addicted to its crema Catalana, cooked with a heavy syrup in an earthenware dish, and further down the coast in Valencia orange juice is added to the mix.

I first ate a version of this flan in the Spanish town of Burriana, home to the Museum of the Orange (see page 23). But the most sophisticated version I have enjoyed was in Seville, where the sweetness of the orange juice was sharpened by a touch of the bitter orange that bears the town's name, and the whole was lightly perfumed with essence of orange flowers.

Serves 4
5 **eggs**
Juice of 1 **Seville orange**
4 large **sweet oranges**
¾ cup **superfine sugar**
¼ cup **orange-flower water**
½ cup **water**
Brown sugar
Ground cinnamon

Preheat the oven to 300°F. Put a deep roasting pan into the oven.

Break the eggs into a large bowl. Finely grate the zest of 1 sweet orange and squeeze the juice of it and of 2 more sweet oranges (leaving just 1 sweet orange). Mix this zest and juice with the Seville orange juice and pour into the eggs. Add ¼ cup of the sugar and the orange-flower water and beat well.

Pour the mixture into a round china or earthenware flan dish about 8–9in. in diameter. Place the dish in the middle of the roasting pan and add enough water to come two-thirds of the way up the dish. Bake for 40–45 minutes, until a skewer inserted into the middle of the custard comes out clean.

Meanwhile, thinly slice the remaining orange. Melt the remaining superfine sugar with the ¼ cup water, and when this syrup is bubbling, slip in the orange slices. Simmer gently for 8 minutes, then let cool slightly.

Preheat the broiler to maximum heat. When the custard is cooked, sprinkle the surface with brown sugar and place in the broiler until the surface is browned and bubbling (be careful that the sugar does not burn—it takes only about 1 minute).

Pierce the surface of the custard several times with a skewer and pour on the sugar syrup in which the orange slices were simmered. Arrange the orange slices over the top and let cool thoroughly before serving, dusted with cinnamon.

ORANGE SALAD & ORANGE-FLOWER-WATER COOKIES

The old quarters of Moroccan towns such as Fez and Marrakesh turn in upon themselves. As you wander through the dark, narrow alleyways of the medina, it is hard to imagine that the vast wooden doors you pass hide secret courtyards and cool, shaded gardens. If you are lucky enough to be invited into one of these households on a hot day, you may well be served a refreshing orange salad, a few cookies scented with the perfume of the orange blossom, and a glass of mint tea.

To make the orange salad

Peel the oranges, making sure you remove all the pith. Cut the oranges into fine rounds, remove any seeds, and arrange the rounds on a circular plate. Pour on the orange-flower water and sprinkle with the confectioner's sugar and half the cinnamon. Chill well before serving sprinkled with the remaining cinnamon and decorated with the sprigs of fresh mint.

To make the orange-flower-water cookies

Preheat the oven to 425°F. Lightly grease a flat metal baking sheet with some butter.

Briskly whisk together the eggs and the sugar, then stir in the orange-flower water and orange zest. Slowly sift in the flour, stirring all the time with a wooden spoon, until you have a sticky dough (it really *is* sticky—don't worry). Dust both the dough and a board with plenty of flour, then, with your fingers, fashion the dough into a cylinder about 2 in. wide. Cut across at ¾-in. intervals and place the cookies on the baking sheet. Bake for 10 minutes, until the cookies just start to color. Let cool slightly before serving with the orange salad.

Serves 4

FOR THE ORANGE SALAD

6 large **oranges**, such as Navelinas

¼ cup **orange-flower water**

¼ cup **confectioner's sugar**

1 teaspoon **ground cinnamon**

2 large sprigs **fresh mint**, to decorate

FOR THE ORANGE FLOWER-WATER COOKIES

2 large **eggs**

½ cup **sugar**

2 tablespoons **orange-flower water**

1 teaspoon finely grated **orange zest**

2 cups **all-purpose flour**

Makes about 16

SPICED PEARS IN HONEY & LEMON SYRUP

Serves 4

1 **lemon**

4 firm **pears**

¼ cup good-quality **clear honey**

1 cup **water**

2 **cloves**

1 **stick cinnamon**

1 blade **mace** or a grating of **nutmeg**

4 **black peppercorns**

There are few fruits that don't benefit from a squeeze of lemon juice to sharpen them, but it's particularly true of apples and pears. Sometimes you simply need that citric acid for practical purposes, to stop the fruit from turning brown, as in a fruit salad. But autumn and winter fruits have a natural affinity that extends well beyond the practical. Try cored apples stuffed with dried lemon zest, bread crumbs, and raisins, and baked; or pears dressed with lemon juice and sugar, stuffed with Stilton cheese. and briefly blasted in a hot broiler.

This recipe for pears simmered in lemon and honey syrup comes from Spain. It is an excellent way of rescuing underripe pears, but does rely on the use of a good honey—a thyme-scented one if you can get it.

Finely zest the lemon and then extract the juice from the fruit. Peel the pears, leaving the stalks attached.

Put the honey, the lemon zest and juice, water, and the cloves, cinnamon, mace or nutmeg, and peppercorns in a heavy-based saucepan into which the pears will fit snugly when you add them later. Place over a moderate heat and stir until the honey has melted. When the liquid comes to a boil, reduce the heat and simmer for 5 minutes.

Now add the pears to the liquid, cover, and simmer for 20 minutes, turning the pears in the syrup several times. Remove the cinnamon stick. Let the pears cool in the syrup for at least 1 hour before serving.

MACERATED ORANGES IN SYRUP

Dessert selections in Italian trattorias always used to feature a bowl of sliced oranges, bathed in a slightly alcoholic syrup. This is a fine dish, which doesn't deserve to be relegated to another era.

Pare the zest from 1 orange, taking care to avoid the pith. Cut the zest into thin strips the size of matchsticks.

Stir the sugar and water together in a small saucepan and place over a gentle heat. Bring slowly to a boil, stirring all the time. When the syrup is boiling, add the thin strips of orange zest, reduce the heat, and simmer for 15 minutes.

Meanwhile, using a very sharp knife, peel the other oranges, making sure you remove any vestiges of pith. Also remove any pith from the orange that you used for the zest. Slice the oranges into rounds, remove any seeds, and lay the slices in a heatproof oval or circular dish large enough for them to fit in a single, overlapping layer.

Remove the syrup from the heat and add the brandy or Cognac. Let stand for 5 minutes, then pour over the orange slices. Wait at least 4 hours before serving—overnight is good.

Serves 4

4 large **oranges**

1 heaping cup **sugar**

1¼ cups **water**

2 tablespoons **brandy** or **Cognac**

ORANGE-MARINATED STRAWBERRIES

Serves 4

1 lb **fresh strawberries**

2 **blood oranges**

Freshly ground **black pepper**

The little town of Nemi, perched high above the deep blue waters of Lake Nemi in hills to the south of Rome, is famous for its fragoli di bosco, *the tiny woodland strawberries that originally grew wild but are now cultivated. If you choose to eat a little bowl at one of the caffès overlooking the lake (and few visitors can resist), you will be offered several serving options: with cream, with lemon juice and sugar, in the local strawberry liqueur, or—my choice—marinated in the juice from a blood orange with a grind or two of black pepper. Try it at home—it even makes out-of-season strawberries taste good.*

Wash the strawberries and dry well. Remove the stalks and cut the strawberries into quarters lengthwise. Juice the oranges. Pour the orange juice over the strawberries, and add plenty of black pepper. Set aside to marinate at room temperature for 2–3 hours before serving.

BLOOD-ORANGE GELATIN

Serves 4

1 pint **blood-orange juice** (this will take about 15 oranges)

2 tablespoons **orange-flower water**

3 tablespoons **gin**

1 envelope **gelatin**

It's odd that gelatin is so often thought of primarily as a children's dessert; not that long ago it was widely regarded as a rather sophisticated dish. This one is definitely for adults only, given the addition of gin.

Mix the orange juice with the orange-flower water and gin.

Melt the gelatin in ½ cup boiling water and add to the juice-and-gin mixture. Pour into a serving bowl and chill well until properly set—at least 4 hours.

Orange-marinated Strawberries

ARROZ DULCE
Lemon rice pudding

Serves 4–6
2 **lemons**
¼ cup **pudding rice**
2½ cups **light cream**
½ **vanilla bean**
1 stick **cinnamon**
1 pinch of **sea salt**
¼ cup **superfine sugar**
2½ cups **whole milk**
Ground cinnamon

Some people think the skin of a rice pudding is the best thing about it, but I don't. I like the way the Portuguese make their rice pudding, in an earthenware pot over a gentle heat. The result is skinless. It is also scented with lemon, cinnamon, and vanilla. Try it for yourself and rice pudding will soon take on a new meaning.

Zest the lemons. Use the lemons in another recipe and reserve a few strips of zest for decoration. Mix together the rice and the remaining zest. Choose a large flameproof earthenware pot. Place it on a heat diffuser (a simple device that fits over the stove ring) on a low heat or turn the heat to the lowest possible setting. Add the rice and lemon zest to the pot.

In a separate saucepan, bring the cream just to a boil with the vanilla bean. Pour immediately over the rice. Add the stick of cinnamon, a pinch of salt, and the sugar, and cook, stirring regularly, for 30–40 minutes, or until all the cream is absorbed by the rice.

Now bring the milk to a boil, remove the skin that forms, and add the hot milk to the rice. Continue cooking, stirring regularly, until all of the milk has been absorbed—this should take another 35–45 minutes. Toward the end of the cooking time, stir more frequently, to stop the rice from sticking to the bottom of the pot.

Let cool and then remove the cinnamon stick and vanilla bean. Transfer to a serving dish and scatter with ground cinnamon (in Portugal this is arranged in decorative patterns). Chill well before serving, scattered with a few shreds of lemon zest.

FIGS BAKED WITH ORANGE

It is a fact that few of the figs we buy are perfect. How could they be? A perfect fig is one just picked from the tree and ours are generally too ripe and overblown or simply chilled to death. This is an excellent way of bringing them back to life.

Preheat the oven to 300°F. Make crosses in the top of the figs and place them in a gratin dish in which they will just fit.

Mix together the orange juice, orange-flower water, and honey. Pour this over the figs, making sure that plenty gets down into the cracks between them.

Bake for 20 minutes. Let cool slightly and serve warm—a thick strained yogurt goes rather well with them.

Serves 4

8 reasonably ripe **figs**

Juice of 1 large **orange**

2 tablespoons **orange-flower water**

2 tablespoons **clear honey,**
preferably thyme-scented

Preparing orange-flower water
The Arabs were the original masters of the process of distilling and it was they who first had the idea of distilling the beautiful white blossoms of the Seville orange tree. The resulting oil is first drawn off (known as Neroli, it is used in perfumery), leaving a highly perfumed clear "water." Useful as an eau de toilette in its own right, this water is also used for cooking in many countries, particularly around the eastern Mediterranean and North Africa, featuring in savory dishes such as Moroccan tagines, in sweets and breads, and in hot drinks such as tea and coffee.

LEMON SYLLABUB

The original syllabub involved a milkmaid milking her cow directly into a bucket of sack or sweet sherry (or even ale on occasion). Left overnight, the milk curdled and the curds became the syllabub.

That recipe does not fill me with delight but this version, based on one by Elizabeth David, certainly does. It is, in a word, wicked. Oh, and I'll add another word: boozy. Don't leave the booze out; it doesn't work without it.

Zest the lemon, reserving a few long, fine twists for decoration, and then squeeze the juice from the fruit. Add both to the cognac and sherry, and set aside for at least 4 hours to marinate—overnight is best.

The next day whip the chilled cream with the sugar until thick. Strain the lemon and alcohol mixture and carefully stir into the cream.

Spoon the syllabub into small glasses and chill well before serving with a twist of lemon zest. A small sprig of rosemary and a candied violet were other traditional decorations.

Serves 4
1 **lemon**
¼ cup **cognac**
¾ cup **amontillado sherry**
1¼ cups **heavy cream**, straight from the refrigerator
¼ cup **superfine sugar**

SAUCES & BUTTERS

Generally, complicated sauces rely on stocks and reductions, and it is better to let professional chefs do the work for you. Certainly, this is not my kind of cooking.

But there are two traditional sauces that are definitely of homely origin—and both rely on the orange. Sauce bigarade for duck, made from bitter Seville oranges, and Cumberland sauce for ham both have well-established histories and remain well worth the (slight) effort. And then there are flavored butters. I cannot resist a chilled pat of parsley-and-lemon butter melting over a rare steak, or a sweet butter delicately flecked with orange over my Dover sole.

Today the kind of liquid I generally call a sauce is produced when I have fried a chicken breast or a fillet of Dover sole in olive oil, added a dash of white wine and fresh herbs to the skillet, swirled it around, and let it bubble a bit. A squeeze or two of lemon or orange juice is rarely amiss. But you don't need a recipe for that.

Gremolada (see page 113)

CUMBERLAND SAUCE

½ cup **water**

Finely grated rind and juice
  of ½ **lemon**

Grated rind and juice of 1 large
  orange

1 teaspoon **arrowroot** or **cornstarch**

¾ cup **port wine**

3 tablespoons **red currant jelly**

Sea salt and freshly ground **black
  pepper**

Although Britain has claimed Cumberland sauce as its own, culinary legend has it that it originated in Germany, gaining its name from Ernest, Duke of Cumberland, who was to become the last independent ruler of the House of Hanover. If you have only ever tasted Cumberland sauce from a jar, you are in for a treat when you make your own. A mixture of orange peel, red currant jelly, and port, Cumberland sauce is (as are so many things in the kitchen) best described by Elizabeth David: "the best of all sauces for cold meat—ham, pressed beef, tongue, venison, boar's head or pork brawn." Or you could eat it just with sausages.

As for this particular recipe, it is a little piece of my own family history. This is the recipe handed down to me by my grandmother but written out for her at my request by her husband, Sidney. I particularly appreciate his addition beside the port wine (written in a small hand, obviously after he had been admonished): "Mother says any wine will do." Well, no, Granny, it won't. But it's a shame that it's too late to discuss it with you.

"Put the water and grated fruit rind into a saucepan and simmer for about 5 minutes. Strain if wished, but if you grate the rinds finely enough they are soft and look attractive in the sauce.

"Add the fruit juices and stir in the arrowroot or cornstarch blended with the wine.

"Bring to a boil and add the jelly and condiments. Cook until clear."

Sidney Woodward (but dictated by Ethel)

My grandfather goes on to note that the sauce can be varied in flavor by adding mustard to taste—but then he was a bit of a fiend with the mustard.

For a more modern approach, you could omit the arrowroot or cornstarch, substitute more port for the water, and reduce hard by fast boiling to thicken. But I like my Cumberland sauce old-fashioned.

GREMOLADA

Chop some lemon zest, garlic, and fresh herbs, and throw them into a rich stew at the end of cooking. This mixture is gremolada, a typically simple Italian idea that transforms a dish—most notably the Milanese favorite of braised shin of veal, osso buco. Precede the osso buco with a saffron risotto flavored with veal marrow and you have my favorite rib-sticking meal for the depths of winter.

But the use of gremolada need not be restricted to osso buco. The gremolada mixture is also very good simply sprinkled over veal, pork, or even robust fish steaks (try it with cod). Gremolada for veal is traditionally made with sage, rosemary, and parsley, but feel free to vary the herbs to suit the dish: chervil and parsley with the fish, for example. (Photograph on page 110)

2 **garlic cloves**
1 small bunch **fresh, flat-leaf parsley**
2 **fresh sage leaves**
1 small sprig of **fresh rosemary**
Finely grated zest of 1 **lemon**
Sea salt

Very finely chop the garlic, fresh parsley leaves, and sage leaves. Strip the rosemary needles from the stalk and chop them finely as well. Mix the lemon zest, garlic, and all the herbs together. Add a little salt—more if you are sprinkling over meat or fish steaks; less if you are adding to an already seasoned casserole.

Traditionally added to osso buco in the last 5 minutes of cooking, gremolada is also brilliant for perking up pork casseroles, or for simply sprinkling over broiled pork chops.

FLAVORED BUTTERS

There is something quite wonderful about a pat of gently melting butter sitting atop a broiled steak or fish. It goes without saying that for this to be successful you must use the best quality butter, unsalted and absolutely fresh. Get a generous hunk of it to room temperature and then mash in your chosen flavorings: orange and paprika for fish; parsley, lemon, and capers for meat (especially good with a gigot of lamb). No sauce could be easier and yet capable of so completely transforming a simple dish.

ORANGE BUTTER FOR FISH

1 **unwaxed orange**

¼ teaspoon **paprika**

5 tablespoons **unsalted butter**, at room temperature

Grate the zest of the orange, making sure that you do not include any pith. Squeeze the juice of the orange and measure 2 tablespoons for use in the butter. Mix the orange zest, the 2 tablespoons orange juice, and the paprika into the softened butter thoroughly. Divide into pats and chill well before using.

LEMON, PARSLEY, & CAPER BUTTER

½ **unwaxed lemon**

1 tablespoon **capers**

1 heaping tablespoon very finely chopped **fresh, flat-leaf parsley**

5 tablespoons **unsalted butter**, at room temperature

Grate the lemon zest and squeeze the juice from the fruit. If you are using capers preserved in vinegar, wash them thoroughly; those preserved in salt should be soaked for about 30 minutes. Either way, dry the capers well and chop them finely.

Thoroughly combine the parsley, capers, lemon zest, and lemon juice with the butter. Divide into pats and chill well before using.

VINAIGRETTES

The name may come from "vin aigre," or sour wine, but there is nothing to say that you must use vinegar in your salad dressings. The acidity of lemon juice marries brilliantly with a fruity extra-virgin olive oil, while the sweeter touch of the orange produces a subtle dressing that is excellent with bitter green leaves, especially if you add a touch of herb-scented honey.

The quantities below are to dress a mix of salad leaves served after the main course. For a more major salad, you'll obviously need larger amounts, but keep the proportion of citric juice to oil about the same. And never make dressing too far in advance, just as you shouldn't dress a salad until you are ready to serve it.

LEMON VINAIGRETTE

2 tablespoons **freshly squeezed lemon juice**
½ teaspoon **sea salt**
6 tablespoons **extra-virgin olive oil**
Freshly ground **black pepper**

Beat the lemon juice with the salt and then slowly drip in the oil, beating all the time, until well amalgamated. Add a generous grind of pepper, pour over the salad, and serve.

ORANGE VINAIGRETTE

2 tablespoons **freshly squeezed orange juice**
1 tablespoon **freshly squeezed lemon juice**
½ teaspoon **sea salt**
1 teaspoon **clear honey**, preferably thyme-scented
6 tablespoons of **extra-virgin olive oil**
Freshly ground **black pepper**

Beat the orange and lemon juices with the salt and honey, then slowly drip in the olive oil, beating all the time until the mixture is well amalgamated. Add a generous grind of black pepper, pour over the salad leaves, and serve.

LEMON & GIN SAUCE

This recipe is based on one in Jane Grigson's Good Things. *She, in turn, attributes it to Kettner's* Book of the Table. *First published in 1877, this is a collection of recipes by the famous restaurateur Auguste Kettner, whose London restaurant still bears his name. Kettner gives the gin as an optional extra to what is essentially a lemon syrup, but Grigson is quite right when she writes "The gin is what matters." It lends added aroma and bite to this delightfully simple sauce.*

Grigson suggests serving the sauce with steamed puddings or baked bananas wrapped in pastry, but I take an altogether simpler approach: I pour it hot over ice cold vanilla ice cream. Nor do I, as suggested, strain the thin strips of zest from the sauce. In fact, they are a bonus with the ice cream, giving both color and texture. Simple yet sophisticated, this makes an ideal dinner party dessert. It goes without saying that you must use the best-quality ice cream.

1 large **lemon**
⅓ cup **sugar**
⅔ cup **water**
2 tablespoons **gin**

Zest the lemon finely and juice it. Put the zest in a saucepan with the sugar and the water. Simmer actively for 15 minutes, until the syrup is nice and thick. Remove from the heat and add the lemon juice: all of it if you like your sauce sharp, as I do; slightly less if you have a sweet tooth. Stir in the gin and return briefly to the heat just to warm through— don't let it boil or you will lose the aromas of the alcohol.

Pour hot over the ice cream and serve. The sauce is also good cold.

PICKLES & PRESERVES

Many of us associate the very act of preserving with another era. Certainly, my memories of making marmalade and drying lemon peel take me straight back to my grandmothers' kitchens. It just shows how quickly we have assimilated the year-round availability of produce. Today we can buy oranges and lemons all year round, of course, so, some people would argue, the need to preserve them is long gone.

But that would be missing the point of orange and lemon preserves. They may have originated as a way of making the fruit available out of season, but they continue to justify their existence today because the very act of preserving creates a unique flavor.

So think of Moroccan lemons stashed in salt, an essential ingredient of tagines; the strips of dried orange peel that give vital flavor to *boeuf en daube*, and homemade lemon curd. As for the most classic preserve of all, marmalade, by all means make it out of season with frozen Seville oranges.

Dried Orange & Lemon Zest (see page 122) and Lemon Slices in Syrup (see page 123)

PRESERVED LEMONS

4½ lb **unwaxed lemons**
¾ cup **coarse sea salt**

Moroccan cooking has many unique flavors, but none more distinctive than that of the preserved lemon. Slivers of these lemons steeped in salt find their way into everything from the cooked salads with which the meal usually starts, through the classic chermoula marinade for fish (see page 34) to the slow-cooked tagines of chicken (see page 61), lamb, and veal. Their long immersion in salt and their own juice gives the lemons an almost honeyed sweetness, which I at least find quite addictive. Make large amounts—they are simple to prepare but need to be left for at least one month, preferably for two or three, before eating and there is nothing worse than running out once you get a taste for them.

Soak the lemons in water overnight. The next day take three-quarters of the lemons and quarter each one from the top to within ½ in. of its base, so that the lemons remain attached at one end. Sprinkle plenty of salt onto the cut flesh and then "close" them up again.

Place some salt over the base of a sterilized preserving jar into which the lemons will just fit, then pack in the lemons, sprinkling with salt as you go. Add the remaining salt and press down on the lemons to release their juices. Squeeze the juice from the remaining lemons and use this to top up the jar—it is extremely important that the lemons are completely covered with juice.

Seal and keep in a dark place for at least 4 weeks before using. The lemons will keep well for up to 6 months.

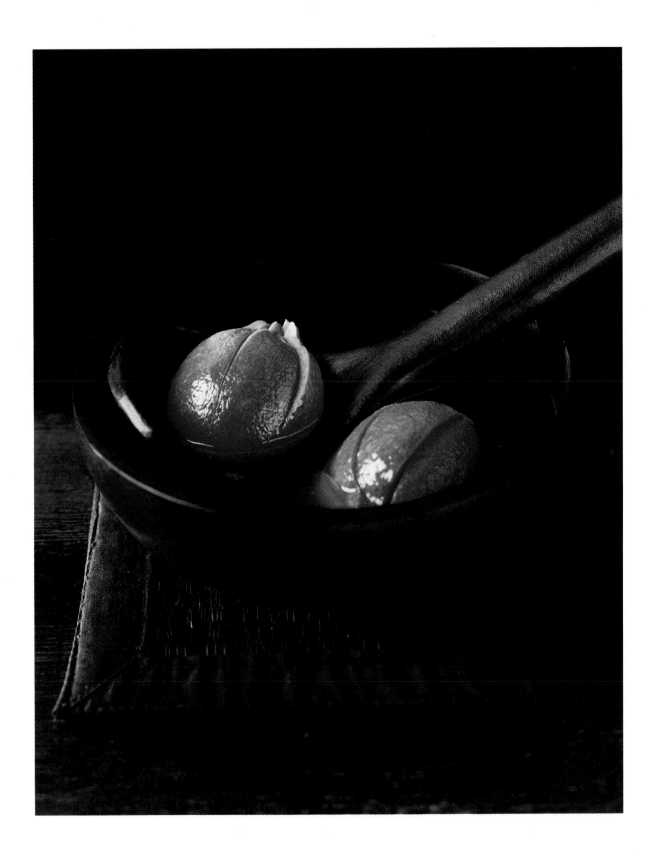

CITRONS CONFITS A L'AIL

6 **unwaxed lemons**
6 **garlic cloves**
1 tablespoon **sea salt**
1 teaspoon **coriander seeds**
Extra-virgin olive oil

If you can't wait a month for your Moroccan preserved lemons (see page 120), then this alternative from neighboring Tunisia is a good choice. This time the lemons are sliced and steeped in garlic, salt, and coriander before being preserved in oil. And you need to wait only one week before eating them—with salads or even just on their own, on good bread.

Wash the lemons well and then dry them. Cut them across into thin slices and remove the seeds, reserving any juice. Crush the garlic cloves. Place the lemons in a large bowl with the crushed garlic, salt, and coriander seeds, and stir well together with a wooden spoon. Set aside for at least 4 hours.

Pack the lemons, layer by layer, into a sterilized preserving jar into which they will just fit. Pour in enough olive oil to cover, shaking the jar to make sure that the oil gets in between the lemons. Seal and keep for at least 1 week before eating.

DRIED ORANGE & LEMON ZEST

Drying orange and lemon zest is very easy, and the results will be much improved if you use unwaxed fruit. (Photograph on page 118)

oranges
lemons

Simply peel the fruit zest into thick strips (too thin and they will fall apart when you use them to flavor casseroles). Bring a large saucepan of water to a boil and add the strips of zest for 1 minute, then drain thoroughly. Pat the zest dry with a dish towel and arrange it on a baking sheet, making sure none of the strips touch.

Preheat the oven to very low (225°F) and leave the zest in the oven for 3–4 hours, until completely dry. I have often seen dried zest hung on a string above the stove, but although this looks attractive, the zest will keep its essential flavors much better if stored in an airtight jar.

LEMON SLICES IN SYRUP

Lemon slices simmered in a sugar syrup: easy to make and excellent to spoon over vanilla ice cream. If you want to dry them, remove them from the syrup after they are cooked and leave on waxed paper at the bottom of the oven set at the lowest temperature for a couple of hours. Eat the dried slices like candy.
(Photograph on page 118)

4 **lemons**, preferably with a high
   ratio of pith to fruit
1¼ cups **sugar**
1¼ cups **water**

  Wash the lemons well, then slice across finely. Mix the sugar and water in a saucepan and place over a gentle heat. Bring to a boil, stirring regularly to dissolve the sugar, then add the lemon slices. Simmer for 15 minutes, then remove from the heat and let the slices cool in the sugar syrup.

    These slices will keep for about 1 month, either moist or dried.

Tales of luxury and intrigue When the papal court moved temporarily to Avignon in the fourteenth century, sugar was still a highly sought-after luxury. It is tempting to think that the candied fruits for which this southern French city is still famous date from that period. After all, twists of lemon peel and tiny whole oranges candied in sugar would have made a tempting bribe during such an era of intrigue and corruption.

ORANGE & LEMON MARMALADE

Marmalade has a long, cosmopolitan history. Britain now claims it as its own, but in fact even the name is borrowed—from Portugal, where the original marmelada was made not with oranges but with quince. Later, the Spaniards and Portuguese perfected conserves of bitter and sweet oranges, and Seville orange marmalade is still the best. As well as Seville oranges, I add the fat, juicy lemons from Amalfi, which come into season at the same time. If you want to experiment with your own marmalade outside the short Seville season, you can freeze Seville oranges whole. This also means you have the oranges at hand for their many other uses.

My recipe makes a thick preserve rather than a more syrupy marmalade and is designed to be used in small quantities—not just on toast but spooned into pork casseroles, melted to dribble over ice cream, and stirred into gravy for duck.

Seville oranges
Unwaxed lemons
Sugar

Note: The fruit should be in a proportion of 2 oranges to 1 lemon. I find that 6 oranges and 3 lemons make enough to fill a 1 quart jar. Also, the proportion of sugar is important to the set.

If the fruit is fresh, soak it overnight in lots of water. If frozen whole, you can skip this stage, as the freezing process softens the flesh and zest.

Put the fruit in a large saucepan or preserving pan and just cover with water. Bring to a boil, then lower the heat so that the liquid just simmers. Cover the pot with a lid set only slightly askew, checking occasionally that there is still enough liquid (but don't add more unless it has totally evaporated).

After about 3 hours the fruit should be completely soft. Carefully lift it out of the pot, reserving the liquid in the pot. As soon as it is cool enough to handle, cut each fruit in half across. Scoop out the flesh and pith from the oranges and discard. From the lemons, remove only the seeds. Chop the orange zest and the lemon zest and flesh roughly into small squares, reserving any juice.

Measure the fruit, and return with the juice to the liquid in the pot. For every 2½ cups of fruit, add 2 cups sugar to the pot. Place the pot over a medium heat and stir until boiling point is reached. Lower the heat and simmer for 30 minutes, stirring every few minutes, until the mixture is thick and dark and looks set. At this stage you can check the set by putting a little on a saucer or even on an ice cube, but frankly, with this balance of fruit and sugar, it is difficult not to achieve a set. Let the mixture cool for about 5 minutes, then ladle into sterilized preserving jars, making sure each is filled to the top. Let cool completely before closing.

CANDIED LEMON PEEL

4 large **lemons**

1 cup **superfine sugar**

¼ cup **water**

In Italy candied lemon peel is used for the famous cakes that are prepared during the Christmas season, but it is also delicious on its own. Do not be tempted to preserve large quantities of this at one time—it never does to overcrowd the pot. Well worth doing in its own right, this is also a very good way to put to use the zest of lemons whose juice has been used for another recipe.

Wash the lemons. Peel the zest off in thick strips, taking care to leave any pith behind. Bring a saucepan of water to a boil and add the strips of lemon zest. Boil for 5 minutes, then drain and refresh with cold water. Bring a fresh saucepan of water to a boil and boil the zest again, this time for 2 minutes. Drain.

Mix the sugar and water in a saucepan and place over a medium heat. Stir all the time until you have a clear syrup. Simmer gently for 5 minutes, then add the lemon zest and remove from the heat. Set aside for about 30 minutes.

Now bring the syrup and lemon zest mixture back to a boil and lower the heat. Simmer gently for about 15–20 minutes, stirring regularly as the syrup reduces. Toward the end of this process, watch carefully—you want to catch the moment just before the sugar starts to crystallize. As soon as almost all the syrup has gone, whip the pot off the heat. Lay the peel out to dry on a sheet of waxed paper for at least 12 hours before sealing in an airtight jar.

SPICED, PICKLED ORANGES

This is an excellent example of how pickling can transform the flavor of fruit. I was only recently introduced to pickled oranges, by a woman who sells her homemade jams, chutneys, and preserves outside an unbelievably picturesque riverside inn. Eaten with a thick-cut slice of properly cured ham, they are reminiscent of pictures of medieval banquets.

Before you start, have ready 1 large or a few small sterilized jars.

Wash the oranges and then slice them across at intervals of roughly ¾ in. Carefully remove any seeds from the flesh. Place the orange slices in a preserving pan or other heavy-based saucepan with the cinnamon, cloves, cardamom pods, black peppercorns, coriander seeds, salt, and brown sugar. Pour in sufficient white wine vinegar to barely cover the contents and bring to a boil. Lower the heat and simmer for 5 minutes.

Let the oranges cool for 5 minutes and then remove the slices, reserving the liquid, and pack into the jar. Pour the hot vinegar and spices on top. Let the liquid cool completely before sealing. Keep a minimum of 14 days before eating; they will keep for several months.

6 large **oranges**

1 **stick cinnamon**

4 **cloves**

2 **cardamom pods**

1 teaspoon **black peppercorns**

1 teaspoon **coriander seeds**

Good pinch of **salt**

1 teaspoon **brown sugar**

White wine vinegar

LEMON CURD

Makes 1 large jar or several smaller ones
2 large **unwaxed lemon**s
1 cup **sugar**
½ cup **unsalted butter**
4 large **eggs**, preferably free-range

Lemon curd, sometimes called lemon cheese, is quintessentially English. It was a favorite of mine as a child, but until I was writing this book I had never actually made it. So it was wonderful to discover that, not only is it relatively simple to produce, but the end result bears little relation to the artificially set and excessively sweet commercial versions.

Lemon curd is at its best reasonably soon after it is made, so I suggest you make it in small quantities and keep it in the refrigerator. I find it so good that I eat it by the spoonful straight from the jar. The more traditional approach is to spread it between layers of sponge cake or on thick, crusty white bread.

Finely zest the lemons and then squeeze and strain the juice from the fruit. Either use a double boiler or (my preferred approach) a glass bowl resting over a simmering saucepan of water on a medium heat, placed so that the bottom of the bowl does not touch the surface of the water.

Add the lemon zest, juice, and sugar to the bowl, and stir well to dissolve. Cut the butter into chunks and add to the bowl a little at a time, stirring all the time, until the butter melts.

Beat the eggs well. Remove the bowl from the saucepan and add the beaten eggs. Stir together well and then replace above the simmering water. This is the tricky bit: You need to cook the curd for about 15 minutes, stirring all the time, never letting it approach a boil or the mixture will curdle. If it looks like it is getting too hot, briefly remove the bowl from over the water. Resist the temptation to raise the heat under the water—the curd does take quite a long time to thicken but when it does, it will do so quickly. And do keep stirring, using a wooden rather than a metal spoon.

When the mixture is thick (and remember that it will thicken further as it chills), pour it into 1 large or several small jars. Cover with waxed paper, seal with a rubber band, and chill well before using.

MARINATED OLIVES

Oranges and lemons have a brilliant affinity with olives, both black and green. Nothing could be simpler than marinating your own olives, and it is worth the tiny effort to be able to produce a fragrant bowl of them with a glass of wine. On the whole, I prefer orange with the small black olives of Provence, and lemon with the fatter green olives that I associate with Spain and Morocco.

BLACK OLIVES WITH ORANGE ZEST

1½ cups **small black olives**

2 **bay leaves**

2 sprigs **dried fennel**

1 teaspoon whole **coriander seeds**

Zest of 1 **sweet orange**

Extra-virgin olive oil

Rinse the olives well and pat dry. Pack them tightly into a jar in which they will just fit, poking in the bay leaves, dried fennel, coriander seeds, and orange zest. Add sufficient olive oil to just cover the olives and keep for at least 1 week before serving.

(Photograph opposite Contents page)

SPICED GREEN OLIVES WITH LEMON

1½ cups **cracked green olives**

¼ cup **freshly squeezed lemon juice**

¼ cup **extra-virgin olive oil**

1 teaspoon **paprika**

1 teaspoon **whole cumin seeds**

2 small **dried red chiles**

½ **preserved lemon**, cut into
  thin strips (see page 120)

Small bunch **fresh, flat-leaf parsley**

Rinse the olives in water. Beat together the lemon juice and oil, and then beat in the paprika. Toast the cumin seeds in a dry skillet, taking care they do not burn.

Pour the oil mixture over the olives and stir well. Add the toasted cumin seeds, chiles, and preserved lemon. Set aside to marinate for 24 hours. Finely chop the fresh parsley leaves and stir in just before serving.

LEMON BRUSCHETTA

I love bruschetta, those slices of bread onto which Italians pile all sorts of savory goodies for antipasti. My favorite toppings include crushed black olives, minced anchovies and garlic, roasted red peppers—strong, sharp flavors that whet the appetite, which is, after all, the intention. Bruschetta toppings are often created from the pickles and preserves in your pantry, making them ideal for unplanned snacks. You need a really good lemon for this dish; the important thing is that there should be a high ratio of zest to fruit. And the bread must be made in good country style as well—chewy and full of flavor.

Place the lemon and unpeeled garlic cloves in a saucepan and just cover with water. Bring to a boil and simmer for 10 minutes. Drain.

Meanwhile, soak the anchovy fillets (and capers as well, if they are salted) in a little water.

Finely chop the lemon, including the zest and pith but removing any seeds. Squeeze the garlic cloves out of their skins and roughly chop the soft flesh. Drain the anchovies and finely chop them; do the same to the capers. Pull the rosemary needles off the stalk and finely chop them, too. Mix all the chopped ingredients together and crumble in the dried chile. Finally, stir in the oil and let stand for about 30 minutes to allow the flavors to mingle.

Toast the bread on both sides until golden. Spread some of the lemon mixture on each slice, top with some arugula, then cut across into manageable pieces. Eat with your fingers.

Serves 2 as a generous snack or 4 as an appetizer

1 large **unwaxed lemon**
3 fat **garlic cloves,** unpeeled
6 **salted anchovy fillets**
1 tablespoon **capers**
1 sprig of **fresh rosemary**
1 small **dried red chile**
¼ cup **extra-virgin olive oil**
4 slices—or, better still, 2 long slices—good **country bread** (pain Poilane is ideal)
Arugula

DRINKS

When I think of lemons and oranges in the context of drinks, I must admit that the first visions that pop into my head are the slice of lemon bobbing about in a gin and tonic . . . the twist of lemon with which I like my dry Martini to be finished . . . the thick chunk of orange I put in my Campari and soda. And imagine a Bloody Mary without lemon juice.

But this is not just about cocktails. Homemade lemonade is the most refreshing soft drink—whether you adopt the English method of preparing a lemon syrup, or the simpler French approach of *citron pressé* (literally, "squeezed lemon"). Elderflower cordial demands orange and lemon juice. And I love a slice of lemon in my tea or some fragrant orange-flower water in my coffee, Turkish style.

Back on the alcoholic theme, there are plenty of spirits that owe their character to these fruits. Gin contains orange and lemon zest alongside the juniper and botanicals; lemon vodka is once again fashionable; and Cointreau is an orange-flavored liqueur at its best diluted with fresh lemon juice and poured over crushed ice. The Italians make lemon liqueur. Perhaps it is time to try your own version.

Fresh Orange Juice with Campari (see page 134)

SPUMATA DI ARANCIA CON CAMPARI
Fresh orange juice with Campari

For 1 cocktail
Campari
Crushed ice
Freshly squeezed **blood-orange juice**
Lemon zest

The bitter aperitif Campari may traditionally be served in its native Italy with nothing more than soda water, but it is a brilliant partner for freshly squeezed orange juice—preferably from blood oranges. It is a truly sophisticated drink.

In their latest book, River Cafe Cookbook Green, *Rose Gray and Ruth Rogers suggest adding the juice of a ripe pomegranate or two or a good splash of the bitter Amaro rabarbo to the drink (the latter addition makes it into a cocktail known as a Milanino). Both are excellent variations.* (Photograph on page 132)

Pour a generous measure of Campari into a long glass. Add crushed ice and top up with the freshly squeezed blood-orange juice. For an attractive finishing touch, add a fine twist of lemon zest.

Iced drinks from desert lands
The word "sherbet" comes from the Arabic "*sh'arbat*," the cooling iced drink based on fruit and sugar syrup of which the Arabs were so fond. When the Moors invaded Sicily, they found a perfect source of ice in the snows of Mount Etna, which Moorish slaves brought down from the heights to make their thirst quenchers. Sicily's water ices, or granitas, for which the island is still famous (see page 98), have their origin in these drinks, the most refreshing of which is made with lemon juice.

CITRON PRESSE

The first time I really lived on my own was for a short and frankly rather frightening period in Paris. It was August (when all sensible Parisians are away on vacation) and I knew no one; but I was determined to indulge myself with the occasional luxury. I think I had watched too many films, to be honest, but I did manage to spend several hours at a time on the Boulevard St Germain dawdling with a citron pressé. *To be charged that much for a glass of lemon juice, sugar, water, and ice was (and remains) an outrage, but there is something about the way it is served that will always charm me.*

Juice the lemons and strain. To serve, the correct form is to first pour the juice into long, tall glasses. Add sugar to taste, a generous spoonful of crushed ice, and water to top it up. Stir (the cafés provide long-handled spoons), and then drink. Simple—and very Gallic.

Serves 4

4 **lemons**

Sugar, to taste

Crushed ice

Pitcher of **ice-cold spring water**

LEMONADE

The real thing: a simple infusion of water, lemon peel, lemon juice, and sugar. Preparing real lemonade requires time but little effort. The result is a syrup, to be diluted with chilled still or sparkling water, to taste, and served in a long, tall glass with plenty of ice, a slice of lemon bobbing on the surface. Nothing beats it on a hot summer's day. This is a seriously grown-up drink, which as dusk falls can be made even more adult by the addition of vodka or gin.

Boil about 2¼ cups water. Peel the zest of the lemons thinly and juice the lemons. Barely cover the zest with the boiling water. Steep overnight.

Meanwhile, mix the remaining hot water with the sugar and heat gently until you have a thin syrup. When the syrup has cooled, mix in the lemon juice.

The next day strain the liquid from the steeped lemon zest and mix it into the lemon syrup. Dilute to taste.

5 **lemons**

2½ cups **superfine sugar**

MILK LEMONADE

Makes about 2½ quarts

5 **lemons**

2 cups **superfine sugar**

1 bottle light, **fruity white wine—**
    Riesling is ideal

6½ cups **whole milk**

lemon slices, to serve

This recipe for a mildly alcoholic and wonderfully old-fashioned milk lemonade is based on one from the irreplaceable Jane Grigson. The milk gives an unusual consistency while the addition of a bottle of wine makes for an adult drink. As Grigson writes, this is the sort of drink you imagine vicars enjoying at summer tea parties on the lawn in the nineteenth century, so the wine really should be a hock.

Roughly peel the zest of 4 lemons, making sure you leave the pith behind and reserving the fruit. Place the zest in a large bowl and just cover with boiling water. Set aside for several hours.

Squeeze the juice of these 4 lemons and then add to the steeping lemon zest with the sugar. Stir well until the sugar has dissolved and set aside overnight.

The next day add the bottle of wine to the lemon syrup. In a saucepan, bring the milk just to a boil, then immediately add it to the wine-and-lemon mixture. The milk will curdle alarmingly—don't worry. Let it cool and then strain through cheesecloth. You will need to strain the liquid several times to ensure that all the curds are removed.

Add the juice of the remaining lemon, bottle the liquid, and chill well. Serve over ice, with slices of lemon floating in it.

ORANGE-FLOWER-WATER TEA

The blossom of orange flowers has long been distilled to produce orange-flower water (see page 107). It is popular in all kinds of North African and eastern Mediterranean dishes. And although the national drink of Morocco is mint tea, an alternative is green tea served with a dash of orange-flower water for perfume. The result is surprisingly like Earl Grey, which, after all, relies on essence of bergamot orange for its distinctive aroma.

In the Lebanon orange-flower water is served after a meal with just hot water; known as a café blanc, this combination is excellent for the digestion. Meanwhile, in neighboring Syria, orange-flower water is sometimes added to the sweet, thick Turkish-style coffee.

Warm a teapot with a splash of boiling water (in Morocco an ornate metal teapot is always used). Add the tea and the sugar, and fill with boiling water. After 5 minutes, add the orange-flower water and stir once. Pour into small glasses, preferably from some height in order to release the fragrance.

Serves 4–6

¼ cup **green tea**

¼ cup **sugar**

2 tablespoons **orange-flower water**

SYRIAN LEMON TEA

Although this Syrian-style drink is called tea, it is really an infusion of water with lemon, just like neighboring Lebanon's café blanc.

Quarter the lemons. Bring the water to the boil in a heavy-based saucepan. Add the lemon quarters, cover, and simmer for 15 minutes. Stir in the sugar and the orange-flower water, strain, and serve.

Serves 4–6

2 **lemons**

3¼ cups **water**

2 tablespoons **orange-flower water**

½ cup **sugar**

LIMONCELLO
Italian lemon liqueur

Makes plenty

6 **unwaxed lemons**

70cl bottle **fruit alcohol**
(80 proof) or good-quality **vodka**

1 cup **superfine sugar**

I first tasted limoncello on Capri. It was a freezing cold day, but it was Easter and the Italians were determined to celebrate, whatever the weather. So they clutched their shot glasses of the icy liqueur to their chests anyway. I was dubious, but then I took that first glug and there it was—distilled sunshine.

Limoncello is nothing more than alcohol infused with lemon zest (not juice) and sugar. It is at its best enjoyed in southern Italy, but you can make a passable version elsewhere, provided that you use unwaxed lemons. However, I particularly recommend making it during the dull days of January and February.

Have a sterile preserving jar at hand. Boil some water and pour enough of it over the lemons to just cover them. Set aside for about 1 hour. Now remove the lemons and roughly pare the zest from them. Place the zest in the preserving jar and add the fruit alcohol or vodka.

Meanwhile, dissolve the sugar in 1½ cups water and simmer for 3–4 minutes, until you have a clear syrup. Let cool, then add this to the preserving jar. Keep the preserving jar in a dark, cool place for 1 month, shaking every day for the first week.

At the end of the month, the lemon liqueur is ready to drink. Strain it into bottles and put in the freezer for several hours before serving—ideally in frozen shot glasses.

SANGRIA

Serves 6–8

2 **oranges**

2 bottles **red wine** (a fruity Rioja or Navarra is good)

¼ cup **sugar**

¼ cup **brandy** (use Spanish—it's cheap and good for this purpose; better still, use Spanish orange brandy)

1 **lemon**

Lots of **ice**

1 bottle chilled **soda water**

The first time I saw sangria being made was not in Spain but in the south of France, in the hills of the Corbières behind Perpignan (an area distinctly Catalan in its history and thinking). It was the day before the village fête and in the local winery the women were busy squeezing crate after crate of oranges into an enormous vat of red wine. To this, I was told, they would add sugar, fine (the local brandy), rum, and Cointreau—plus a few lemon slices.

At first I reacted with an uncomprehending stare when I was told this was the ideal drink for the ladies because it was "lèger"—light. But sangria does not have to be a killer. Made with a fruity red wine and a cautious hand on the brandy bottle, diluted with soda water and lots of fruit, it is an excellent summer thirst quencher.

Squeeze the juice from the oranges and reserve 1 squeezed fruit. Mix the orange juice with the wine, sugar, and brandy. Roughly chop the reserved orange and add to the mixture. Place in the refrigerator to marinate overnight.

The next day remove and discard the orange pieces. Thinly slice the lemon and float the slices in the sangria, with lots of ice. Dilute to taste with the soda water.

ELDERFLOWER CORDIAL

To make the refreshing cordial, you will need flowers from the elder tree (which grows in the mountains of North Carolina, west to Arizona, and north into Canada) and freshly squeezed lemon and orange juice. This recipe is from my stepmother, who lives in Dorset, in England, where elder is common and the delicate, lacy flowers are also deep-fried in batter—exquisite. Serve the cordial diluted with sparkling water over ice, and a slice of lemon—although my father occasionally sneaks a shot of gin into the mix.

25 **elderflower heads**

3 **lemons**

3 **oranges**

5 tablespoons **citric** or **tartaric acid** (this makes it keep for longer; if omitted, it will still last well, refrigerated, for about 2 weeks)

1¾ cups **sugar** to every 2½ cups liquid

Gather the elderflowers when in full flower, but before the pollen falls when they are shaken. Check for blackfly and avoid flowers growing near roads and agricultural pollution.

Slice the lemons and oranges. Put the flowers into a large container with the lemon and orange slices, the citric acid, and the sugar. Pour over 5½ pints boiling water and let soak for 24–48 hours, stirring occasionally to dissolve the sugar. Strain through cheesecloth, and bottle (sterilize bottles for a longer life). Dilute with water, to taste. The cordial may be frozen for later use.

AGUA DE VALENCIA
Water of Valencia

On hot summer evenings this potent cocktail is served in big glass pitchers in the cafés that line the square overlooking Valencia's cathedral—a favored hangout for local youth. Essentially Buck's Fizz laced with a kick of vodka and a dash of Cointreau, Agua de Valencia should be enjoyed in a group of keen party-goers—and probably kept for a Friday or Saturday night.

Serves 6–8

4½ cups **orange juice**, freshly squeezed or a good-quality juice from a carton

¼ bottle **iced vodka**

1 shot glass **Cointreau**

1 chilled bottle **cava** (Spanish sparkling white wine)

Mix the orange juice with the vodka, Cointreau, and Cava, and serve. If you prefer, you can use gin instead of vodka. I favor the latter, but I have seen it served with both.

INDEX

Note: all recipes contain oranges or lemons or both. Listed under "orange" and "lemon" are general entries plus only those recipes whose titles start with one or other of these fruits.

First published in 2001 by

Conran Octopus Limited

a part of Octopus Publishing Group

2–4 Heron Quays

London E14 4JP

www.conran-octopus.co.uk

Managing Editor: Emma Clegg

Project Editor: Ann Kay

Editor: Barbara Horn

Creative Director: Leslie Harrington

Designer: Mary Staples

Photo-shoot Home Economist: Louise Pickford

Photo-shoot Food Stylist: Wei Tang

Proof-reader and Indexer: Michele Clarke

Recipe-tester: David Morgan

Production: Gaelle Lochner

British Library Cataloguing-in-Publication Data. A
catalogue record for this book is available from the
British Library.

ISBN 1 84091 215 4

Color origination by Sang Choy International,
Singapore

Printed in China

Author's Acknowledgements

With thanks to: Claire Wrathall for
commissioning the book and all at Conran
Octopus for seeing it through the process;
Vincente Abad from the Orange Museum
for sharing his infectious enthusiasm for the
orange, and José from the Valencian Tourist
Board for joining in the spirit; my parents for
introducing me to the lemons of the Amalfi
coast and Capri at a tender age; Mic and
Chris for providing an inspirational spot in
which to start writing the book; and, as ever,
Jonathan for being official taster and a lot
more besides.

Picture Acknowledgements

The publisher would like to thank the
following photographers and agencies for
their kind permission to reproduce
photographs in this book.

6 Anthony Blake Photo Library

8 Jonathan Blair/Corbis

9 Alan Keohane/Impact

10 Tim Hall/Axiom Photographic Agency

11 Chris Caldicott/Axiom Photographic
Agency

12–13 Museu de la Taronja, Castellón, Spain

Every effort has been made to trace the
copyright holders; we apologize in advance
for any unintentional omission and would be
pleased to insert the appropriate acknowl-
edgement in any subsequent edition.